THE PRODIGAL PROJECT

THE PRODIGAL PROJECT

journey into the emerging church

Cathy Kirkpatrick

Mark Pierson

Mike Riddell

First published in Great Britain 2000
Society for Promoting Christian Knowledge
Holy Trinity Church
Marylebone Road
London NW1 4DU

Third impression 2001

Scripture extracts are from *The Holy Bible, New International Version*

British Library Cataloguing-in-Publication Data
A catalogue record for this book is available from
the British Library

ISBN 0281 05250 6

Printed in Great Britain by
The Cromwell Press, Trowbridge, Wiltshire

CONTENTS

We dedicate this project to the lovers, dreamers, dancers,
outcasts, subversives, prophets, weavers, misfits, players, artists,
healers, mystics, activists, questioners, laughers and cooks,
who have been bruised but keep following Jesus.

And our heartfelt thanks to Andrew Lórien,
who toiled in the engine room of the CD-ROM, without reward
or chocolate fish, and by whose grace things work as they should.
You are honoured among us.

ACKNOWLEDGEMENTS

Thanks to Alister Kitchen (cartoons), Arthur Amon (chants, poetry and visuals), Cityside Baptist Church acapella group, Sean Donnelly (music), Brenda Stone (who knows good words from bad), Robyn, Sarah, Raychel and Isaac (for constantly reminding me that I am loved despite who I am), all Citysiders ever (the best little church in the Universe), Tom Sine who told me I should write, alt.worship communities around the world. Without you all this production would never have risen above the slough of despond and I would have drifted beyond the fringes of the faith a long time ago. You hold the future of the church in your hands and imaginations. Thanks to my co-authors and friends Mike and Cathy (wonderfully assisted by Andrew). Mike has held my hand through controversy and conflict. He inspires me with his courage and conviction; humbles me with his insight and faith. Any time I work with Mike is always hugely satisfying. A real mate. Cathy, with her enthusiasm and stunning work on the CD-ROM has constantly encouraged me to believe that the Project might actually happen. Her green hair phase was an inspiration to me.

Mark Pierson. Email: mark@cityside.org.nz

Thanks to Mark who started me on the crazy journey into alt.worship, and who has remained a shining example of what the word 'friend' might mean. I owe him a great deal more than I can ever say. And to Cathy, who found me by trawling cyberspace. She weaves magic wherever she goes, and cares abundantly. And Andrew the pirate/wizard. To Soul Outpost – especially Jen, Peter, Agnes, Leanne, Emma, Jim and Ian – you have given me a home for dreaming. A nod to my wider community – Simon and Anet, Steve and Lynne, Pete and Tess, Dave and Pat, Sally, Jonny and Jenny, Tom and Christine, Tim and Merridie, Fuzz and Carolyn, Martin and Meg, Jif and Rhi, Malcolm and Meryl, Dave. We have to stop meeting like this. Thanks to the Catholic community for embracing me so readily, and to the Theology department at Otago University for trusting me with students. But most to Rosemary, Matt, Polly and Kat, for knowing me and still loving me. I can't believe my good fortune in being part of such a family. Oh yeah, a tip of the hat to the Big Three – your kingdom come.

Mike Riddell. Email: m.riddell@xtra.co.nz

It is difficult to know who to mention here … will I be thanking you, or implicating you? Firstly, thank you Sue and Pete Kaldor, for encouraging me to write stuff down and for being incredibly supportive friends. Thanks Huw Luscombe and Hilary Stewart for your unique friendship and wonderful poems. And to Tim Ollis, for all the years – The Cave, before and beyond – and for all the fish, of course. Mark, you threw a lifeline across the Tasman to me, from the Parallel Universe to the church of caffeine … for this I am eternally grateful. Mike, the friendship you have offered me in c-space and at table is more precious to me than I can say. Thank you to the people of my House: to Allison and Rick for all your love and care, and to my beautiful husband Andrew, the best man in the world. And finally to all the people of Café Church. The journey continues, may God go with us.

Cathy Kirkpatrick. Email: fish@geko.net.au

PREFACE

It's hard to say how this project started. Whether it was round the dinner table amid banter and good food, or whether it was born out of that strange silence which follows a worship event which has made you cry again, who can say? We were all in it together, that much is certain. And we all egged each other on, so that before we knew it we had started off on something which was always going to be beyond us. And just as well. If it weren't for the 'beyond', what would there be worth saying?

We knew from the outset that it would be a project, in the sense that it would never be complete. The experiences and reflections contained here are generated by a stirring which is not of our making. We could neither contain it nor define it. The best we could hope for was a gathering together of what Cathy likes to call 'bits'. But we felt someone had to make a start somewhere. All of us have despaired as we have seen so many good people falling at the stumbling block of the institutional church. We hoped that we might catch some before they turned out the lights altogether.

Each of us has felt that despair ourselves, despite our continued links with the established church. But by the grace of God, we have discovered a source of hope and excitement among newly emergent communities of faith. Small fragile groups, who have dared to exercise creativity and imagination in their pursuit of Christ. We have seen and felt and heard and experienced things there which we wanted to share with others. And so the project began.

From the outset we wanted it to look good. We hoped that the medium would convey some of the message of creativity, participation and fun. And so emerged the idea of a book containing a CD-ROM, where people could go beyond reading to immerse themselves in a realm of colour, surprise and interactivity. Cathy (a graphic designer) and Andrew (a programmer) have put in the hours of love and work to make this part of the dream a reality.

We also knew that the project had to be a joint effort. It needed to express one of the foundational things which we have learnt; that the way ahead lies in relationship and participation. So despite the fact that sections of text have continually navigated their way between Dunedin, Sydney and Auckland, we have made of it a joint work. A couple of times we assembled on different sides of the Tasman Sea, during which celebrations we sometimes remembered to do some work on the book.

There is so much more we'd like to say. Things we'd like to show you. Qualifications we'd like to make. But it is, after all, only a project. It will be the people who make use of it who will shape it and determine what it might yet become. Our hope is for the future of the Christian movement; that it may once again become a vibrant representative of grace, mercy and love. That may require a little time and attention, and perhaps even prayer.

> I'm lost. I'm trashed. And somewhere deep inside I'm raging. I am wild with angst and frustration at all the stupidity and blindness, at all the backflipping and mindbending. I want to get my chainsaw out. I want to explain … And I know that if what I am feeling is worth anything, then I must begin that careful journey of communication.
>
> ckp

There's something interesting happening in the Christian community across the Western world. Very quietly and unobtrusively, one group of believers is growing on a daily basis. Soon the numbers will be such that they can't be ignored. Who are they? They're the Christians who don't go to church any more. The ones who've given up altogether. A recent email from a friend anguished over these missing faces: 'I tell you, so many of my Christian friends – the ones who were going to put the church to rights, the ones who were going to fight for the cause of the disenfranchised believers – are giving it all up now.' Not the faith, as such. Most of these people still believe in Jesus, and struggle to live a life of discipleship. But they do it on their own, away from congregations and church structures.

Why are they leaving? For all sorts of reasons, some of which they find themselves hardly able to articulate. Most of them feel that church is not their 'home' any more. But for every Christian who used to attend church but now does not, there are many more who grit their teeth of a Sunday and endure a service for the sake of making some obvious commitment to the community of Christ. They feel isolated, weary, out of place and frequently angry, but they also feel they have no option but to hang in there. If you identify with one of these groups, then we are writing for you. We write out of our own years of frustration and struggle with the institutional church, but also out of our profound joy at having discovered life within/beyond it.

Our intention is not to critique the established church. The target is too easy, and it has been done too many times before. We are not trying to disenchant people with existing forms of worship. For those who like things just the way they are, we say 'God bless you'. Our intention is to speak to those in pain and grief, and to hold out some hope and encouragement. We believe that there is still transforming power in the gospel of Christ, and that the Spirit is still at work in the life of people. And we have caught a hint of something new that God is doing around the fringes of the church; something we long to share with those who are ready to hear it.

The things we have to say are broken and fragmentary, like our own lives. We have no package to offer, no ten–step programme to effective worship. We don't even know what we think until we say it, and even then it might change by next week. But we feel constrained to speak. Because our words are inextricably woven into the threads of our journeys, we share a little of them here.

Mark's Story

At Easter 1990 I attended the 50th anniversary reunion of my high school. Twenty years had elapsed since my year group had finished at this school – enough time for some nostalgia to seep through, yet not so much time that we were dead or too infirm to manage to get together. There was a large turnout of old friends and acquaintances.

As the weekend and the many stories unfolded I became more and more intrigued. Our discussions increasingly centred on issues of spirituality and faith. Georgina was very familiar with the supernatural, having experienced powerful demonstrations through the occultic activity of her warlock partner. Karen had seen her broken life and relationships transformed through involvement with the healing power of crystals. Again and again I met people actively involved in, or open to, spiritual searching and experiences. Not one of them was looking in the church. In fact several had begun searching there and rejected it as unhelpful. What hit me hardest was knowing that these people would not find what they were looking for in *my* church either – and I would not invite them to try because it would add to their problems, not solve them.

These were ordinary New Zealanders. People who shared the same hopes and dreams that I did for a fulfilling marriage, good friends, drug-free kids who would make a positive contribution to society, satisfying work … People looking for some answers to the big questions of life, and I wouldn't invite them to my church, and I was the minister.

As I drove home from the reunion my tears determined that I would find some way of growing a church that these people would find helpful and supportive in their search for spiritual reality. The reality found in a relationship with Jesus Christ.

> Most of us have been burned by the church (I can show you the scars), and have struggled to find a new identity and place of belonging where it's possible to be normal and Christian at the same time.
>
> Mike

New Year's Eve 1998 was equally formative. A family in the very different church I am now a part of, had rented a house in a beautiful, sparsely populated beach in the hot sun of summer in northern New Zealand. They'd invited anyone from our church to join them any time. It was evening and 25 or so young adults were lounging around reading, playing cards, chatting, philosophising, with Jeff Buckley's 'Grace' playing in the background. As I looked around the room at people I cared deeply about, I realised how significantly different the scene was to any I had experienced in any other church community – even at the age of 20 or 30. Here in this group of young adults who were followers of Jesus were all of the characteristics that in the 1970's I had been told were 'of the world' and definitely not 'of Christians'.

There was enough beer, wine and spirits to stock a substantial liquor store, several people were smoking cigarettes, 'bad language' could be heard from time to time, and the camping arrangements were mixed gender, although not necessarily sexual. While this struck me as a significant contrast to the environment I grew up in, I doubt that one of these people would give a second thought to any of the issues. Alcohol, cigarettes, language, male–female relationships were just not considered the important issues and certainly had nothing to do with whether or not a person was a Christian. What is important for these people is integrity, reality, spirituality, and relationship (in the sense of friendship). The issues have moved.

That night I realised why so many branches of the mainstream church were irrelevant – measured and found wanting – to these young adults and to so many like them. Too often the Church was answering the wrong questions;

questions these people weren't asking. Answers that only served to widen the gap between faith and reality rather than integrate the two.

I was glad that I was on a journey with a community of faith that is trying to figure out what the right questions are. A group of people who are willing to ask questions that may not have answers; people who accept me as I am and still love me; people who live life to the full and yet realise that it has a dark and painful side and can't be lived uncritically. It is sad and unfortunate that this openness to questioning and the search for a robust and real faith that can cope with the realities of a tough life is often interpreted from the outside as liberal and non-Christian.

Cathy's Story

It must have been at least August 1989. Things had had a few months to really blow apart. I was sitting at the back of church. Not the back row. The back row was too obvious. I left it for those who didn't really want to be there, and were prepared to show it. I wanted to be there; although I hadn't been for some time.

This was the church of my youth. At 15 I had walked through its doors after some camp or other, and forgot to stop. During the years 1983–1989, I scarcely ever missed a night.

We were asked to stand and sing. I didn't really want to stand, much less sing. But I stood, and dug my fists deep into my pockets, and watched the words for a while, then looked at the backs of my friends.

I remember an image forming in my mind. A knife. Being thrust into my ribcage. And again. I wondered at this, and even more as to why the knife was clenched in my own hand …

> I don't want numbness – I guess it's what I fear the most.
>
> Rick

That knife would twist between my ribs for six years to come. I could hear my life-breath escaping, as I felt myself slowly bleeding away.

The previous year, 1988, had been a year of horizons expanding, in which I often had to re-cut my case with God: how do we go on in relationship in the light of this experience/idea/influence/person? December began the years of hell. Something had been set in motion, and the acts of the great play struggled across the stage of my life, until the death of my father in June 1993 brought to an end the stream of crises. The ceasing of the body blows allowed for a season of recovery, restoration, and the rebuilding of resources and energies.

I remember a single scene from a brief sojourn at Sunday School. I remember sticking tiny bits of wallpaper on a card. I remember something about sins being washed away. I thought of them looking like scars on the skin. Sunday School meant wearing that pink woolen knitted dress, and coping with the Clarke twins who were always mean to me. I boycotted the situation, and somehow everyone in my family stopped attending church. My mother prayed with me at night: 'Gentle Jesus meek and mild, look upon this little child; pity mice implicitly . . .' I begged God to keep nightmares from my sleep, which plagued me until my teens.

My brother was the visible Christian in the family. He was much older than I, and when his years as a camp–goer gave way to the years as camp director I received an invitation. At age 10 I attended my first Christian holiday camp. I was amazed by the song books and guitars; by the games and the catering. I learnt my first Bible verses – Gen 1.1, John 3.16, Rev 4.11. I listened to the testimonies of the leaders. I participated in a drama in which a piece of white wool was strung around a door frame in the shape of a heart. Someone knocked at the door, and a Jesus figure opened the door and beckoned inside. After camp I secretly asked Jesus to come into my heart, and be my friend. I told no one.

The year after I finished high school, I became worship leader at church, with a newly formed music group, and had begun my time leading a succession of Christian camps and houseparties. In 1987, I was distracted from my second year of study at art school by a group of teenagers: a fellowship group called 'Elevators'. In 1989, I was leading (and hosting in my apartment), a cell group for Year 12 students, and a home group of my peers. This was the end.

The circus of family crises had begun, and I was slowly dying. I spent that year extracting myself from leadership roles as I experienced slow emotional and spiritual death. I was spiralling. Our church youth worker observed that in times of crisis most people press more closely into the household of faith, whereas I was doing my best to withdraw. I reached a stage where I could not physically get myself to go to church. I dreaded the people; not the individuals, but the phenomenon of the mob. I dreaded the enthusiastic greetings: 'CKP! How are you?!!'. I had absolutely no idea what to say. Things were both really good, and really really bad, at exactly the same moment. In the end, I hadn't the energy to say anything. I avoided people beyond my immediate household. I wondered why no one was asking me about my absence from church ... one friend suggested that it was beyond anyone's questioning that I might be choosing to stay away: 'They just assume that you're off reading to the 5,000, or something...' Oh.

And so, we arrive back at that night in the second back row. I felt strange. I had brought my world with me. My emotional, situational, spiritual world. I wasn't happy, or bright. I wasn't energised, or even very cooperative. I learned a lot about what not to say to fringe-dwellers in those years. I had stopped reading the Bible regularly ages ago. My prayers had been reduced to: 'Oh God, o God, ohhh GOD ... you know ... you know what's happening ... I don't know whether you wanna change anything, but please, keep me alive ...'. Oh God oh God oh God, as I wept into the washing-up, as I fell onto the floor of my room, as I knelt down in the shower ... o God. Things were so black, I was so black, that I'm not sure how I survived those years. Grace, and a few good friends. I was hitting the bottom, and from there I saw things I had never seen.

I now know that God never lets go of his end. The subconscious doctrines of works, where I can only know God as well as I live up to all the good Christian standards, slowly faded. My faithlessness didn't stop God's care. I would sit on the living room floor with a handful of teenagers – I would look at them and know that they were all so much more faithful and zealous than I. I prayed that my state would not cause them to stumble. I looked at my life, and could find no signs of obedience to God, and yet, I remained . . .

In 1990, I finished my studies, quit my four part-time jobs and began attending a full-time career; changed where I was living and with whom I shared, and arrived on the doorstep of a brand new church. I had hardly even visited another congregation since I had become a churchgoer. This was weird. I tried to get into it; I even joined a home group. Pretty soon, people began to see around my black clothes, leather jacket and dramatic haircut . . . hey, who's this kid? Hey, kid, come over here ... I did my best to live below their expectations. Oh, I'm sorry, you've mistaken me for a responsible person.

Before I left that gathering, my passion for fringe-dwellers and for troubled youths got the better of me, and I had made a stumbling attempt to form a fellowship group for the wandering teenagers of the parish, and began doing voluntary graveyard shifts at a drop-in centre in the city. I was in no real shape to do it, and after a couple of years with the multinationals and more personal crisis, I sold out everything, and limped to Europe.

After Europe, I moved to Glebe, to a warehouse with my friends. 'The Cave' was a kind of meeting place for our friends, our community. There was always coffee on the boil, and raisin toast for the traveler. The healing had begun. In 1994 I ventured onto another camp – strictly to cut vegetables. At Christmas I traveled with a Christian band on 'mission'. I took photos and lugged amps. I was edging tentatively back into the soup, the group, the vibe, the new tribe. I considered risking a connection with a wider Christian community ... yes, church.

I wanted a church in the inner city, somewhere nearby. I saw a notice on the front of a building, making it known that the congregation of Glebe Uniting had moved from its sandstone home on the other side of Glebe to this three-story brick job. That made me wonder ... gutsy call for a people to move like that ... what could it mean? The others in my household also needed a new gathering, so one Sunday morning (yes, morning ... there was no evening option) we staggered down from our lofts, and stumbled down the back alley ... to church. That was beginning of the long voyage which led to the creation of Cafe Church and beyond.

I had made contact with God before I had made contact with 'church', or discovered the phenomenon of communing with other Christians. The Bible and prayer had always been important. Attending and leading camps had a deep impact on me – friendship, discussion, meals, fragments of life lived together. The journey took me deep into the heart of church, and out again. Along the way I learned that God is not only present and at work within the halls of religion – God is out there ... out here. The friendships I have forged along the way have cut deep: these people are engraved on my soul. Our friendships have continued beyond the walls within which we met. Even in my darkest moments there remained with me my friends and my God.

Let me say here that being a part of the formation and ongoing life of Cafe Church has been one of the most exhilarating, challenging, painful, enriching, frightening and creative times of my life. I stumble on. God have mercy.

> I'm not angry at church, or harbouring resentment; I just don't need them. My own unique circumstances and life experiences brought me to where I am now, often entailing extended periods of angst coming to terms with all of life's adventures en route (i.e. losing parents, lack of roots, being divorced, gay, nomadic, etc.)
> Peter

Mike's Story

This is one of those stories which sounds too bizarre to have actually happened, but it did. A young girl lived with her family next door to a Baptist church. Her parents were not churchgoers, but they made use of the Sunday School to get their daughter out of the house on a Sunday morning. Each week she would attend Sunday School, and then stay on for the church service which followed. Family life was not pleasant, and she enjoyed the welcome relief of a different group of people who seemed much 'nicer'.

> I am no longer 'at home' in the trad church … Did I say that? – hey, I'm the flamin' minister!
>
> Rev. Anon

The church was charismatic, and on one particular Sunday, there was the usual long bracket of choruses at the beginning of the service. A very worshipful atmosphere developed as the congregation continued to sing songs over and over. Eventually, after a particularly moving chorus, a silence fell over the assembled people. It was one of those times in which worshippers are caught up in the presence of God, and hold their breath in expectation of some prophecy or exhortation from the Lord.

This time, however, the silence gave way not to any encouraging word, but to the sound of screaming from next door. There was the unmistakable noise of a woman being beaten; a succession of wailing and weeping interspersed with the thud of fist on flesh. The young girl, together with the rest of the congregation, listened in horror. She recognized the voice of her mother crying in anguish, and knew that once more her father was erupting in violent anger. She waited in anticipation, to see what would happen.

The worship leader was tense. He had planned carefully the sequence of songs to lead to this very point, where people might 'break through' into the presence of God. And now instead, the whole atmosphere was being destroyed by this unwelcome intrusion of the outside world. He did the only thing he could think of; he led out in another song of praise. The congregation welcomed the opportunity to move on and drown out the ghastly sounds assaulting their ears. As they sang, the worship quickly shut out the noise from next door. The incident stayed with the young girl for the rest of her life, though she did not understand until much later why it made her so angry.

In many ways the story is expressive of my own increasing dissatisfaction with the worship of the Christian church. My own background is Baptist and charismatic, and I can understand the scenario from both sides; that of the church and that of the young girl. Increasingly, however, I have found myself identifying with that tortured adolescent. Alone, frightened and disillusioned. Not only unable to connect my outside life with the worship of the congregation, but finding that the so-called worship was being used positively to exclude that wider experience. She and I both hoped for more from the community of Christ, and were disappointed.

Increasingly I became aware of the great gulf separating the different streams of my life. It seemed that to enter a church building was to pass through into a different dimension, where everything was different and strange. In the ecclesial setting, none of the music I listen to was played, little of the language I spoke was used and none of the literature I read was mentioned. The sermons did not address any of the issues I struggled with or cared about. Nor was there any chance for me to discuss, to argue or to question. And yet that is the only way I know to process things for myself. As the initial romanticism of the Charismatic movement faded, I found myself moved to boredom and frustration by worship.

Later, when I became a Baptist minister responsible for a congregation, things improved somewhat. I found myself among a lively group of people with passionate concerns both for the contemporary world and the arts. Our services included contemporary readings (where a selection from contemporary literature was read), and the highlight of a 'free-for-all' time after the sermon, in which people could wrestle, discuss and pray in a community forum. There was a rich diversity of music, from rock to gospel to Bach to chanting in Latin.

Yet still I found myself dissatisfied. The elements of the service all fitted into a traditional pattern. We still sat in pews. The whole thing was still led from the front, and took place in a building largely unused from week to week. I was bored myself, which is not good when you are the minister. People came because of the community, and loved the experience of being together. But it was as if we had to endure a set format of meeting in order to be entitled to meet together. As a church, it was better than most other church communities that I have experienced, but it was still remote from my experience of ordinary life in many respects.

Rescue came in the form of a letter from my long-time friend and colleague, Mark Pierson. He had been interested in some experiments in alternative worship in the United Kingdom, and now dared to dream that we could attempt a new model for ourselves in New Zealand. Mark was looking for a team of people

> In order to pioneer new forms of church we have to self–consciously step outside mainstream tastes, which always accept the status quo. We have to engage with the leading edge of our culture in order to reconnect the creative engagement that should never have been disengaged.
>
> Spike

willing to commit themselves to an open-ended process, and I jumped at the opportunity. The result was Parallel Universe, a free-wheeling worship community which exploded onto the Auckland scene some six years ago. That story can be told elsewhere (and probably should be), but for me it was life-giving and revolutionary.

For the first time in many years I found myself excited about worship. I couldn't get to sleep at night for dreaming and planning and wondering about coming events. I would come away from our team sessions buzzing with enthusiasm. My whole world was transformed, literally. I could no longer listen to music or watch a movie or read a book without thinking about their significance for worship. Every time I entered a public building I would assess its possibilities for hanging screens and placement of projectors. And best of all, I would come away from worship events tired but deeply satisfied, caught up again in the majesty of the Christian story. It was like jumping naked into a lake after years of not being able to touch water.

The one gift which had brought about this profound liberation was deceptively simple; that of permission. Through the grace of others I had been allowed to dream again of what church might be, instead of playing the game within someone else's space and rules. Together we began to respond to God as the people we were, and with the resources which formed our place and culture. At times the freedom was overpowering, and we probably abused it in our enthusiasm. But if so, it was a transgression brought about by many years of ecclesiastical captivity. And our own release flowed on to those who joined us in the venture.

> It was SO boring. And oh, that horrible man! I just wanted to stand up and SCREAM!!
>
> My Mum

By meeting God outside the confines of church buildings, church language and church culture, we touched base with a huge group of people engaged in a journey of spirituality. Some of them were bored church members, some of them were people hurt by the church and no longer involved, and some of them had never been in a church before and were unlikely to ever. They shared a fascination with the possibility of God, and a hunger for authentic spiritual development. These people wanted to discuss, to examine, to ponder as they picked their way through the unreliable topography of life. Our biggest problem became that we could not get rid of them after a worship event - they wanted to stay and talk.

I have now moved from Auckland to Dunedin, and from Baptist life to Catholicism, but the exhilaration of new worship continues through my involvement with a group called Soul Outpost. We have discovered a great family of people across the Western world who are involved in similar ventures. It has been exciting to realise that our own experience is not isolated, but part of something much bigger which is happening in many places. It is audacious in many ways for us to raise our voices as we are doing in this book. But we do it out of a recognition of the profound hunger and distress being experienced by many people like ourselves. We don't have answers. But we do have stories, experiences, learnings and resources. Perhaps these may help others along the Way.

The Grief for What We Have Become

There are many possible reasons why people might get sick of church; some better than others. A recent study in NZ of why people leave the church turned up some interesting answers. Most of those interviewed were quite articulate about their reasons for doing so. When pastors were spoken to however, the majority suggested that the drop-outs were either experiencing a crisis of faith or had personality problems. While in certain cases this may be true, the reaction is a classic example of 'blaming the victim'. The church accepts no responsibility for the increasing tide of disaffection, but rather wants to call into question the integrity of those who have been alienated.

This book is not anti-church. If anything it is a call to renew our hope in what the church might yet become. We want to grab the attention of those drifting toward the fringes of the established church (or already beyond it) and suggest that giving up may be premature. We hope to persuade any who will hear that the current crisis of the church in the West is a time of great opportunity, and that underneath all the anxiety and discomfort there is the hint of God's restless stirring. We dare to believe in a future for the community of Christ against all the statistical odds. If we were against the church, we would not bother.

But that said, there is within the established church in the West a 'sickness unto death'. The problems are many, common, persistent and deeply-entrenched. There will be no quick solution; no programme to be implemented which will 'fix' things. We can anticipate a long and rocky road of reform, with all the pain and conflict which change and transition brings. Some may find themselves already too tired to begin. We hope to convince you that it is worthwhile to hang in there and be part of the movement of God.

To all those who are already grieving from the experience of church, we want to say thank God. Thank God that you have moved past the numbness of so much ecclesiastical life; thank God that you have retained enough vision of the kingdom of God to be moved to anguish by the church; thank God that your suffering tells you that your spirit is still alive. The beginning of change lies in dissatisfaction and grief. Your disappointment and anger is the call of God to you to resist and transform the reality you have inherited.

> The church experience is for me the least enjoyable part of being a 'Christian' … tolerable, heavy with expectation, light on genuine connection.
>
> Jo

Grief can easily become sick. If it turns in on itself, and gets locked in anger and withdrawal, it can be corrosive and destructive. Or it can be the first sign of a coming change, just as winter strips bare the trees for a coming spring. We are people of hope, who have seen an early blossom out of season, and are crazy enough to believe that it may be a sign of things to come. Our lives continue to be filled with a great deal of pain because of our living within and commitment to the established church. But our dreams lie with that which it might yet be.

If we share our own experiences of alienation within the halls of religion, it is not to promote discontent, but to help others know they are neither alone nor misguided in their own negative reactions. You have heard already a little of our stories. The following are some of the things we have felt along the way.

BOREDOM

While boredom can be a sign of arrogance and disdain, it can also be an indication of a total lack of connection and meaning. So many words, so many sermons, so many choruses, so many earnest entreaties, so many 'solemn assemblies' of the faithful, and not an ounce of meaning to be found. How many times can you count things, or wander off on daydreams, or draw pictures on the notices sheet before you begin to give up on the whole enterprise? I've often sat in services and been tempted to shout or cause mayhem simply to provide some point of interest within proceedings. Sometimes that has been when I've been the one conducting the service!

ISOLATION

Loneliness is bad enough at anytime. But when you feel it most acutely in the gathering of the people who are supposed to be your sisters and brothers in the faith, it develops a particularly mocking tone. There have been times when I have felt like a visitor from another planet. I look around the congregation, and everyone appears to be having a good time except me. They all seem to understand the language and be moved by the music. So why is it that I remain on the outside of it all, like looking through a plate glass window into a restaurant?

What is wrong with me? Many times I can't even pinpoint exactly what is wrong with the whole event of church. I simply feel desperately alone and sad, and cut off from all those around me.

DISCONNECTION

You know how it is when you understand a smattering of words in a foreign language; just enough to catch little bits of what's being said, but not enough to make sense of it. That's how it sometimes feels in church. I understand words like 'Jesus' and 'baptism' and 'grace', and even more difficult ones like 'atonement', but something about the way they are put together to make a worship service leaves me feeling that I've missed some vital connection. On the other hand, most of the bits of life that I'm most passionate about never get a look in at church. Some friends of mine put it this way:

> We can't enter into worship on Sunday and embark on a pedestrian wade through a four hymn sandwich without setting aside the "holy" experience of a bar we spent last night in, listening to a funky soul singer, and sipping Irish coffee. We find worship an unconnected experience when we realise how alien it seems to recall the spiritual energy and gospel motifs we found in experiencing the latest version of Romeo and Juliet at the movies. And we often want to cringe in church when we sing a melodic jingle about loving Jesus, when we think of our souls soaring as we play U2's complex "Pop" album loud on our CD player at home.

PASSIVITY

I've been guilty at times of wondering what difference it would make if I weren't there at all. The whole show seems to have an impetus of its own, regardless of the people are supposed to be the 'participants'. Most of what goes on concerns a person or group of people up the front. I feel like a member of the audience, sitting in my lonely wooden pew watching a show which is not especially engaging. From time to time there are things I would like to say or questions I'd like to ask, but there seems no place or opportunity to do so. Too often I take my passions and pains home with me, and nobody else in the 'community' knows they exist.

MISUNDERSTANDING

A few years ago, when I left my job teaching theology to Baptist candidates for ministry, one of the students gave me a baseball cap as a leaving present. On the front, it declares 'Jesus loves me'. Under that, printed on the peak where it's a little more difficult to read, it says 'but everyone else thinks I'm a wanker.' I feel like I need a hat which says 'I really do love Jesus.' That might help to inform people who imagine that because I drink wine or sometimes swear or listen to Radiohead or get angry or watch dodgy movies, that I can't really be a Christian. Having to explain yourself and justify your experience becomes exhausting after a while. At times I feel more acceptance outside the church than inside it.

ANGER

Yes, I'm afraid it's true. Occasionally I get very, very angry with the way the church is. I get angry as an insider. I am angry that we have managed to take something so vital and passionate and life-giving as the gospel of Christ, and make it into what it has become. I get angry about all the hypocrisy and pretense and judgement and moralizing which goes on in communities of Christians, and more angry still that I contribute to it. Mostly I recognize that my anger is an inverted form of hope for something more and different, but not always. There have been times when I have stayed away from churches because they fuel my anger, and I've considered it more gracious to remain absent.

Starting Anew

These then are some of the things we have experienced in the church at worship. You will either recognize them or not. If not, it's probably best to put this book aside now. But if they strike a chord with you, and you find your heart leaping that someone else has put into words what you've been feeling, then we want to invite you on a journey of transformation. But first we simply want to say to you that you are neither alone, nor mad, nor sinful to have experienced these things. You are someone in whom the longing for grace has not been subsumed by the numbness generated by institutional religion. You are no better or worse than anyone else who is part of Christ's church, but you may become a bridge to faith for those who are to follow.

We live, as the Chinese would say, in interesting times. Some of us have found a way of giving expression to our faith without violating our sense of who we are. It is patchy, tenuous and transitional. Those who have begun in different corners of the world have reached out to each other and established a network of people involved in what is variously called the 'alternative worship' or 'new worship' movement. That sounds more grandiose than it is. In reality, it's simply a group of people who have been experimenting with doing new things, rather than giving up on church altogether. As Charlie Irvine has said, we've done it as a matter of survival. We're not trying to prove a point to anyone, or to compete with more traditional patterns of worship. We're just trying to function as people following Christ.

The Prodigal Project is a resource kit for people who have enough energy left to begin anew. We have no plan for what you might make in your own context and among your own people. We sincerely hope it will be unlike anything ever created before, and unique to your own setting and community. All we have to offer is a collection of learnings from our own paths, which may or may not be helpful. Our one hope is that it might result in people being able to more authentically worship and respond to the amazingly adventurous and irrepressible God made real to us in Jesus Christ.

It's like here I am and I like dancing — but dancing on your own can get a bit boring and lonely so I look for other people to dance with and eventually I fetch up outside a building and the sign on the door says Line Dancing Academy. Well it's dancing, and there are a lot of people and they look pretty happy and they say they can teach anyone ... So pretty soon there you are, 3rd row back, 7th in, going through the motions. And your memory of your own dance and how it used to come through you is getting hazy but on some level you know that your ability to hook into wherever that dance used to come from has been fractured. And you just wonder if you took the boots and hat off and walked outside the Academy and walked on for a bit, maybe you'd start to feel that again.

Nancy

This chapter has some heavy-duty stuff in it. It gets a bit more serious, because it's trying to make sense of fairly serious changes in the course of human existence. I guess we could have skipped it, and you can if you find it too pointy-headed or theoretical. But the reason for having it here is so that you can take some comfort in the knowledge that at least part of the reason you feel so disoriented is because everything is changing. Every now and again it helps to be able to see the big picture, and find our own place in it.

> The organized church structures are the brothel house of religion. I visit them because there are still some innocents among the debris. And their scandal is my scandal. But I will not prop them up.
>
> Mike

Introduction

'Don't it always seem to go, you don't know what you've got 'til it's gone.' So sang Joni Mitchell many years ago, with sweet poignancy. And surely it does seem like the truth. Many people these days are grieving the loss of a way of life that has disappeared almost as quickly as the 'paradise' she mourned. We feel nostalgic for something, even when we can't find the words for what it is that's missing. Like the characters in George Orwell's *1984*, we have vague memories that things may have been different once. But even the future has become past for us.

For better or for worse, we have the privilege of living through one of those periods of history when the world really does change, substantially and irretrievably. The general sense of dislocation felt by so many is a valid indicator that the ages are moving under our feet. The upheaval is such that, as Yeats[1] had it, 'the centre cannot hold'. There is a good deal of anxiety felt in our global society at present, as the things which once were fixed begin to betray our long-standing trust in them.

Over the last half of the twentieth century, the great ship of Western culture has been listing, terminally holed below the waterline. Why should a cultural synthesis which has endured for centuries suddenly begin to founder under our feet? It's not hard to identify some of the causes, but in the end none of them is sufficient to explain the events. There is an essential mystery in the turning of the tide of the ages, which Christians might want to describe as the activity of God in history. It is something we must have respect for rather than attempt to control, much as seafarers learn to honour and read the ocean.

The fact that the mid-point of cultural transition coincided with the turning of the millennium has fuelled apocalyptic distress in the wider community. It is not necessary to be a social commentator or historian to be aware of deeply troubling disquiet. It 'feels', especially to those who straddle the ages, as if everything familiar has fallen around our ears, and we have woken in foreign territory populated by Barbarians.[2] A great deal of the stress present in Western urban communities is due to this seemingly non-specific dis-ease.

The church, as one cultural vessel among many, finds itself in troubled waters. On the one hand, the ship of the church is itself foundering in the cross-currents of cultural transition. And on the other, it has become a sort of hospital ship, attracting refugees from a former era who find in it hope of return to more familiar waters. To employ a much-overworked analogy, there is a good deal of rearranging of the deckchairs, not to mention angry arguments on the bridge. Meanwhile, some distressed passengers are leaping overboard, preferring their chances in the open sea.

To be a Christian in these times is not easy for a Westerner. To be a churchgoer is even more difficult. There is something of a crisis of confidence, as previous modes of response to the world prove increasingly inadequate. In such times, it is important that we as the body of Christ do not turn on each other, nor be too quick to allocate blame for the difficult waters we have encountered. There have been many attempts to locate the bogey: the failure of the clergy, the selfishness of the laity, the lure of materialism, the subversion of 'humanism', the activity of demons, the lack of evangelism or the absence of the Spirit.

None of these is sufficient to explain current problems. Rather, much of the malaise the church is experiencing is simply the result of its participation in the wider cultural shift occurring in society. We have woken to find ourselves in 'exile', despite having no clear memories of getting there.[3] It is, naturally, a strange and troubling place to be. It will be important to grieve, and to express the pain at that which has been lost. But it is also important to try to understand what it is that's different about this new place, and how we might learn to sing our songs in a foreign land.

The Back of the Whale

It is part of Maori[4] wisdom that when one sees the back of the whale breaking the surface of the water, you can be sure that the rest of it is not far away. The whale which rises in our own historical seas is that of postmodernity. The nature and advent of postmodernism is a topic which attracts much confusion and debate, and perhaps it is safer to speak about the emerging culture. While commentators are divided over postmodernity,[5] most are in agreement that Western society is in the midst of cultural transition. If we were to suggest that a major movement such as the current one takes about a century to be carried through, and that the shift began in the 1950s, it becomes evident that the process is well under way.

In the present climate, it is easier to talk about what is passing away, rather than that which is coming after (i.e. 'post') modernity. It may well be that we are just beginning to see the back of the whale breaking the waters. It is too early to describe in great detail what this surfacing leviathan looks like, but it is too late to deny its presence or proximity. Part of the difficulty of these times is that we live 'between the ages', when the previous culture of modernity still holds sway and power, but the emerging culture is present with vigour. The following discussion is an attempt to sketch both that which is passing and that which is coming to be, in order that we might understand the spirit of the times.

Behold, the Old is Passing Away ...

Fundamentally, the earthquake which has generated the current cultural tsunami is a revolution in the way we 'know' things. As such, its roots lie in the area of philosophical discourse, and the particular field of epistemology. Suffice it to say here that the work of thinkers such as Kuhn, Polyani, Toumlin, Lyotard, Rorty and others has changed forever the structures of human knowledge.[6] Most people will be blissfully unaware of the seminal writings responsible for the shift. But more recognizable are the cultural and social outworkings and symptoms of the revolution.[7] Any listing of them is selective and open to dispute, but the larger picture will be more important than the detail. Here, then, are the signs of the old order.

PROGRESS

There was a time, particularly in the 1950s, when it seemed that humanity had unlimited potential. This was the culmination of centuries of scientific methodology being applied to the structures of life. All problems were potentially solvable, given enough time and money, and the sustained application of reason. Technology fuelled a 'Gee Whiz' admiration of the white-coated midwives of a new future, in which all would be clean and efficient. The Western world, long regarded as the vanguard of this coming age, was supremely confident and optimistic.

It is difficult to say how the balloon became punctured. The long shadow of nuclear annihilation made clear to all of us the dark side of technology. The Vietnam war demonstrated that the world's best-equipped and scientifically endowed superpower could not overcome a dedicated peasant army. Ecological awareness grew as we began to take stock of the way in which our 'progress' had poisoned the planet on which we rely for life. Urbanization created dislocation, poverty, racial tension and crime. AIDS made the gleaming gods of medicine appear impotent.

Together these forces and others deflated the sense of unfailing certainty that the world could be shaped and tamed in accordance with human desire. The doubt regarding our ability to relentlessly improve living standards extended to a new sense of uncertainty as to whether such a goal was even desirable. 'Progress' could no longer be assumed to be attainable, sustainable or worthwhile. In the late twentieth century, visions of the future lost their purity and became decidedly dark (e.g. *Bladerunner*).

OBJECTIVITY

One of the key principles of science has been that of the impartial and detached observer, who takes careful precautions not to interfere with the results of their research. Since Descartes, 'pure' knowledge has been based on the disconnection of the knower from the known. Objectivity was essential to the process of discovery and the reliability of the data gained. In the universe of science, both the possibility and necessity of objectivity were posited until comparatively recent times. There was a sharp distinction between the 'hard' facts of scientific knowledge gained through objective observation ('Barometric pressure is 1005 and falling'), and the 'soft' unreliability of other more casual means of human knowing ('I don't like the look of the weather').

Recent developments both within and outside of science have eroded this distinction, and indeed the whole mythology on which 'detached' and objective knowledge is based. The *possibility* of observation in which the 'subject' has no effect on the 'object' has been thrown into doubt by developments with scientific disciplines such as quantum physics. It is now generally recognized that there is no access to phenomena in their 'raw' state, i.e. unaffected by human observation. Thus there is no scrutiny of reality in which that which is analysed remains uninfluenced by the presence of the person doing the recording.

Another challenge to the 'myth of objectivity' comes from perceived results of such an approach to the natural order. When reality is treated as an 'object' for human understanding and manipulation, it seems that abuse follows. Environmental disharmony and tragedy is the apparent legacy of our industrial-scientific relationship (or lack of relationship) to the world. Adopting an 'I-It' attitude to nature allows a callous and exploitative interaction, to the detriment of ecological health and ultimately to life itself.

The function of the objectivity myth as a means of holding and wielding social and cultural power has recently been understood. Feminist critiques, along with other voices from the margins, have exposed the way in which 'fencing' knowledge is a way of excluding unwelcome groups and streams of experience. For several centuries, a largely white male academic heterosexual professional group has regulated admission to acceptable knowledge, and hence to social power. This hegemony of truth has now been subverted well and truly by the insistence of the marginalized that they gain access and participation in the pursuit of understanding. They have succeeded in claiming the validity of alternative and seemingly 'subjective' realms of knowledge.

RATIONALISM

For much of recent history, to label an argument as 'irrational' was sufficient to dismiss it from consideration. In fact, the common lore of our chauvinist heritage at one time used this accusation to disparage the contribution of women. The ability to be rational was considered the great achievement of modernity; the power which raised us from the mire of superstition and ignorance of earlier ages. Descartes' famous declaration, 'I think, therefore I am,' has been treated as something of an agenda which will rescue us from chaos. It has taken until the end of the second millennium to understand the limits of rationality.

It's not that rationality is wrong or unnecessary. However, there has been a growing understanding that it represents one approach to relating to the world, which on its own is insufficient to make sense of life. In particular, resistance has grown against *rationalism*: the elevation of reason to a position of authority which it has no right to occupy. The Bible has always recognized that the mind must take its place alongside heart and strength and soul in the pursuit of God, and as we will argue, the overthrow of a narrow rationalism may be beneficial to the nurture of faith. There are important aspects of reality which the mind struggles to process, and at such points we may gladly confess its inadequacy, while not dispensing with its service entirely.

LINEARITY

The dominance of reason has helped to produce a particular method of coming at things, which might be termed linearity. Probably a legacy of the printing press, this approach to life and knowledge gives the impression that everything has a beginning, middle and end, and that the correct means of approach is to move sequentially and in a linear fashion from start to finish. Everything in the West, from scientific dissertations to orders of worship, has been influenced by this way of reading and processing material. So much so that many people will feel profoundly disoriented if the 'natural order' of progression is tampered with.

Computer technology and the advent of the World Wide Web have contributed to the collapse of linearity, or at least its claims to universality. The ability to work with information in a more intuitive fashion has revealed both the excitement of working in that way, and the inadequacies of the more conventional approach. Bypassing the sequential ordering of rationalism has been found to break up the tyranny of reason, and opened people to new possibilities and experiences. It has also demonstrated that people have the capacity to absorb data at many different levels concurrently, and are in some ways more at home in doing so.

TRUTH

For a couple of millennia, whatever philosophical or theological debates may have consumed the Western experiment, there has been agreement at one point. That is, that the truth is out there. The assumption seems to be that we have been consistently and progressively getting nearer to it with all of our debates and discoveries. Now, for the first time, comes the suggestion that the truth does not exist at all, at least in the way that we have thought about it previously. Claims to possession of truth are now regarded as claims to power and superiority. There are no 'truths' in the absolute sense available; instead we have socially constructed agreements as to what is true 'for us'. Preoccupation with overarching truths (metanarratives: grand stories which explain everything) or absolutes is an attempt to retreat from the essential tentativeness of human existence.

While the relativism of recent times does not necessarily discount the possibility of truth beyond subjective appraisals of it, the *de facto* force of encountering many different views has been to discount the validity of all of their certainties. Truth has not disappeared from the map entirely, however, but simply been reinterpreted. The new understanding is perhaps best expressed in the title of a Manic Street Preachers' album: 'This Is My Truth; Tell Me Yours'. It conveys the personal nature of truth, together with the belief that it is possible for multiple truths to exist, even if they are contradictory. Obviously such an attitude is regarded as anathema by many, including Christians, who have dedicated their lives to a concept of truth which is eternal, absolute and knowable. It is not surprising that they feel deeply distressed in response.

REALITY

Even more disturbing is the loss of reality. Reality has been the solid ground which we shared in common. So much so that people who were regarded as having lost contact with 'reality' were often confined in institutions. The scientific age in particular has reinforced the belief that reality is external, fixed and able to be perceived. It is something which we must encounter and adapt ourselves to in our journeys through life. Reality was something you could learn about, shape a little, but ultimately rely on.

Unfortunately, even this sacred ground has come under attack. People who were marginalized by the way the world was (such as women, blacks, gays) began to question the basis of reality. They were able to demonstrate that reality is socially constructed. That is to say that what is commonly perceived as the outside world which everyone encounters, is actually a complex consensus of belief. So, for instance, the certainties of what men and women are 'designed' to do turn out to be quite different when viewed from other perspectives. Furthermore, this being the case, it must be possible to construct alternative realities which can claim just as much validity as those with deeper historical roots.

INSTITUTIONS

There have been certain prominent institutions which have regulated society in recent history. These include established bodies such as the monarchy, the military and the church, as well as entrenched patterns of behaviour like marriage. The late twentieth century saw the erosion of many of these foundational structures of civil life. Even where they continue to exist, they have lost their power to constrain the lives of citizens by right. The great historic institutions have lost the allegiance of the population at large, at least in the West. They stand as quaint reminders of a past era; monuments of a vastly different age. Unfortunately, for many people the Christian church is to be counted among these relics.

> On my journey, the more distance I gained between myself and my church roots, the less able I became to comprehend that this institution, *en masse*, could be worth propping up. Not with any malice or bitterness, but just through observation and getting on with life.
>
> Willie

As the winds of freedom and personal choice have blown through the decades, increasing numbers of people have felt less inclined to allow others to exercise authority over them, or to tell them how to live their lives. Even where there is allegiance to the aims which a particular body seeks to promote, there is less willingness to offer subservience to the institutional structures of that body. It is pointless for ailing institutions to berate their followers or even to seek to accentuate their own worth and importance; such attempts succeed only in further isolating those who make them from contemporary culture.

MORALITY

Ethical principles have usually been a function of some deeper view (more or less religious) of how people fit in connection with the cosmos. It is not surprising, then, that when big visions (metanarratives) are failing, ethical certainty should also diminish. The absolutes which at one time provided the foundations of moral behaviour are crumbling, causing a loss of moral confidence and a great deal of confusion about how one can establish the difference between right and wrong. Conservatives and fundamentalists of every kind condemn the apparently immoral behaviour of youth, and call for a return to 'traditional values'.

It is not only the loss of absolutes, however, that has engendered ethical bewilderment. Scientific and technological advances have meant that our power to achieve certain ends has outstripped our ability to determine the value of doing so. Many of the moral decisions which must be made are ones which are new and unprecedented in human history, and so ethical traditions are of limited help in making them. Genetic engineering is only one realm where a great deal of expertise is necessary to even understand what the issues are. And certainly, without a common core of agreement as to central values, it is difficult for societies to legislate morality.

There may be a temptation for Christian people to blame the current societal discord on a departure from 'religious values', and to suggest that the world has 'gone to the devil'. However, this is a simplification which only leads to defensiveness and reactionary fear. While there may be legitimate concern for the preservation of good in the face of evil, calling for a return to the past is as misguided and impossible as the wish of the people of Israel to go back to their captivity in Egypt, rather than face the unknown challenges of foreign territory. Our task, as theirs, lies in crossing the border and discovering God in a new place.

... and the New is Come

Postmodernity is not simply the dying of the old. This is the time of transition, when a new and previously unseen creature is emerging from the chrysalis. It's too early to say exactly what it is that is coming into being, or to map its precise form or colour. But we can offer some hints and predictions; a few glimpses beyond the veil of the cocoon. There is already talk in the West of the 'emerging culture', and participants in it know that it feels different from what went before, even if they find it hard to articulate in what ways. The following, then, are broad brushstrokes. The detail will follow from those who have the benefit of retrospect.

JUXTAPOSITION

Perhaps the clearest insight into the difference which Postmodernism represents is to be gained through the idea of juxtaposition. This means putting things side by side with each other which don't normally co-exist. Not only is this a feature of postmodern art; it is a symbol of the entire culture in its acceptance of proximate difference and even contradiction. Diversity is not feared; if anything it is valued. Opposing symbols, perspectives and beliefs are allowed to meet and interact, rather than being regarded as mutually exclusive. Tension is viewed as creative, with the possibility of opening up previously unperceived elements of experience.

Related to juxtaposition is a new talent for 'reading' quite diverse elements simultaneously. Whereas a child of modernism prefers to watch a television drama from beginning to end, later progeny love to channel-surf in a seemingly random and disconnected way. Multiple tasking is not just a term for computer processing, but describes the ability to absorb disparate sources of information or experience without needing to concentrate on one to the exclusion of others.

In a similar way, people are learning to live their lives out of a wide range of paradigms, which may have elements that suggest internal contradiction. It may be possible, for example, for someone to be a vegetarian, but to sanction hunting as long as those doing it eat their own kill. Or to have a strong morality regarding the non-pollution of the environment while being a committed smoker. Ethical views which an earlier generation would regard as totally chaotic find reconciliation in the lives of participants in the emerging culture.

RELATIONALITY

When, many years ago, I was training to be a minister, I recall being told that it would be inappropriate for me to form any friendships with people in the congregation. Somehow, it would be thought of as 'unprofessional'. This attitude is one that belongs with the compartmentalized world of modernism. Thankfully it seems to be on the way out, along with the 'objectivity' and 'culture of experts' which caused it. Now there is a growing hunger for relationship and community, paradoxically at the same time as those qualities become difficult to find. There is, however, a new appreciation of the essential *relatedness* of people, animals, environment and cosmos.

Through coffee lounges, email groups and urban subtribes, there is a fresh longing to connect at some deeper level with the mass of humanity who otherwise remain anonymous. Being woven into the fabric of a community of people is of course nothing particularly new. The distinctive part of postmodern relating is that it is not given by birth or circumstance, but by and large is chosen. It produces groups that are consequently more fluid than earlier more formal communities, but it also allows greater freedom and potentially more depth of relationship.

PARTICIPATION

Some centuries ago the old world of authority ruled over by powerful hierarchies eventually gave way to democracy, where all citizens contributed to the shape of society. In contemporary culture, however, the formal mechanisms of democratic decision-making are themselves regarded as remote and exclusive. There is a new call for participation; genuine involvement of people at the grass-roots level, where they may begin to shape their own destiny. A vote is not nearly enough. What is required is the sense of each person having a genuine contribution to make, and allowance made for their particular gift to be exercised.

Established institutions are not good at coping with this new approach to common life and decision-making. It appears to be chaotic, time-consuming and open to abuse. Those who are used to exercising power as if it were their natural right become frustrated when the group process allows even the most reticent participant a chance to contribute. The goal, however, is not *efficiency* but *inclusion*. The process is a reaction against the way in which people (especially those marginalized through nonconformity with norms) have previously been excluded and their voices silenced.

> The most important thing about the group is that we're like a family to each other. So we're real with each other rather than painfully polite (which occasionally causes friction) but we do care about each other …
>
> Sue

SPIRITUALITY

Less than fifty years ago, the consensus in scholarship was that the Western world was in an advanced stage of secularism (living without gods). Writers spoke confidently about the end of religion and the triumph of science. The explosion of interest in spirituality over recent decades has therefore come as something of a surprise to commentators. Looking back, we can perhaps speak of an experiment of secularism which appeared as a temporary blip on the graph of human development. It was ultimately no more sustainable than attempts to restrain human intellect. It was inevitable that there would eventually come an eruption of that which had been suppressed under the sway of the Enlightenment.

Today we have an explosion of interest in spirituality, but it looks very different in shape from any of the traditional 'religions'. Everywhere it seems people are captivated by questions of meaning and the deeper significance of life. Over the table in coffee bars, in the dialogue of movies or among groups chanting by the seaside, there is discussion of the spiritual elements of human existence. God is back on the agenda, but Christians should not get prematurely excited about the fact. There is no enthusiasm for association with institutional forms of religion, and indeed a great deal of suspicion about them. One of the sad facts is that people alert to the reality of God never even consider that a church would be a place to help them on their journey. Even more tragic is that an increasing number of Christians might be tempted to agree with them.

In many ways this aspect of postmodernity is similar to the situation which faced first-century Christians encountering the culture of their day. Then as now the question was not whether there was a spiritual dimension to life or divine beings, but more what the nature of that realm was. Do we speak of gods or God or Godde? Are angels the same as spirit guides? What's the difference between Transcendental Meditation and prayer? Are aliens emissaries from the spiritual world? There is no doubt that the emerging culture is not only open to but fascinated by questions of this kind. Christians face a world in which it is possible to tell their story, but only if they are also prepared to listen to the experiences of others.

HOLISM

If one of the effects of modernity was to split the world apart into atomistic fragments for the purpose of study, then the reaction of postmodernity is to bring these fractured elements back together again. Everywhere there is a concern with the *connection* between different aspects of existence, rather than seeking to compartmentalize and classify them according to their difference. The most obvious arena where this trend is becoming evident is that of health. At one time medicine was rigorously concerned with individual organs and their functioning, giving rise to such blasphemies as 'the appendix in bed thirteen'. Now there is a dawning recognition of the interconnection of every aspect of a person's life with their well-being. This is evident not only in the rise of alternative therapies and 'natural' cures, but also in the willingness of doctors to spend more time listening to their patients' stories.

The ecological movement is an expression of holism, in its recognition that human life cannot be lived 'over against' or apart from the natural environment, but needs to find harmony with it for the long-term sustainability of life itself. The so-called 'Gaia hypothesis' regards the entire planet as a single organism, with each eco-system vitally connected to the others in the maintenance of earthly health. Even in science itself, which has for some time been more interested in particulars than wholes, it seems that new discoveries are producing evidence for the connection of various phenomena in the universe. Previous models which might have imagined life consisting of discrete marbles banging up against each other are being replaced by a more web-like vision, in which everything is joined to everything else.

ROMANTICISM

It may be that we are entering on an era coloured by a new romanticism. The world of 'hard facts' and 'bottom lines', while still in ascendancy in many places, is being quietly challenged by the perennial quest for beauty, love and meaning. Among young people, there is less interest in lifelong careers or even long-term goals, and a corresponding surge of enthusiasm for more creative pursuits such as poetry, art and self-expression. The materialist utopia has proved itself to be curiously unsatisfying, even at the point of its greatest accessibility. Now many people are beginning to regard work as a short-term instrumental activity to allow them to pursue the creative endeavours which are their real vocation.

It is not, however, an uncomplicated or naive romanticism. Alongside it is a seemingly contradictory cynicism. This functions as a protective force-field to guard that which is personal, creative and highly valued, just as the shell of an egg creates a hard exterior for the embryonic life which is within. The revolution of love against progress which had its early flowering in the 1960s, is resurgent at the beginning of this new millennium. It raises issues of purpose, satisfaction and significance in the pursuit of the human journey; all topics on which the followers of Jesus might usefully join the discussion. After all, if nothing else, Jesus is a crucified romantic. The resurrection aids our recognition that God, too, is a romantic.

PLAY

One of the defining characteristics of the emerging culture is a light-handed playfulness. Some of the features of the new world which disturb parents most and are potentially dangerous, are regarded by those who indulge in them as experimental investigation with the sole purpose of enjoyment. These include such experiences as drug use, body-piercing and even bisexuality. The normal developmental phase of pushing the limits is supplemented by an almost nihilistic lack of boundaries, so that any area of human activity is open to exploration. Indeed those that have been proscribed by society in the past are regarded as potentially the most interesting to revisit. There is often no conscious attempt to desecrate, however; rather the motive is one of frolicking in forbidden fields.

New technology is regarded by many in the emerging culture not so much as instrumental to scientific or industrial progress, but more as helpful in playing better games. Computers can create cool graphics and animations, and the internet is good for developing cyber-relationships. Food, drink and conversation are consumed with enjoyment and a lack of concern for the constraints of time or finance. A playful attitude to life leads to a different ordering of priorities. To the inhabitants of modernism, the attitude of the new generation appears hopelessly disconnected from reality. But conversely, the players in the emerging culture regard career plans and 'getting ahead' as dull distractions from the joy of existence.

IMMEDIACY

There are two aspects to the immediacy which shapes the emerging culture. The first and most obvious is the 'fast food' syndrome; people are impatient with any delay. The whole concept of delayed gratification is a foreign idea to those who find a few seconds wait in front of the computer screen frustrating. Along with the accelerating speed of the culture is a corresponding reaction against anything which slows access to it. The second and more subtle influence of immediacy has to do with vitality and connection to immediate experience. It was the lack of this which led Kurt Cobain to commit suicide. In the early days of undiscovered music-making, Cobain felt some exhilaration in the experience of musical performance, particularly in front of a crowd. Later, he found it hard to reach the intensity of feeling, despite being a superstar. His suicide note read: '... I don't have the passion any more ...' The lack of direct intense participation in experience was enough to make him despair of life itself. If immediacy could no longer be attained, there was not much point in carrying on.

Postmodern culture is very much in-your-face; loud, fast and aggressive. It doesn't allow withdrawal to some secure buffer zone of reflection or analysis. The object is to be truly present and involved in the experience, whether it be sex or music. If necessary, drugs are a means of enhancing the intensity of the event. There is no preamble or post-mortem; the immediate present is sufficient in itself, detached from any wider network of meaning, value or interpretation. Consequently the culture is largely experiential in orientation, and certainly has difficulty in relating to any purported reality which doesn't have an experiential element. There are obvious implications here for Christianity.

Problems for the Church ...

The church is struggling within Western culture. Sure there's pockets where everything is going swimmingly, and the First Century Apostolic Revival Centre is proud that its membership graph is on the way up. But overall, the scene is not good. To put it in a nutshell, the church in the West is at best surviving, and at worst dying. Probably, if you've read this far, you're one of those who already knows that something is amiss, and don't need convincing of the fact. The sad thing for many of us, who love Christ and try to love his church, is that we struggle ourselves to find meaning inside the institutional form of it. It's not the sort of place we want to invite our friends to.

Some of the problems are the normal ones of institutional life, like inflexibility or power games. But a number of the deeper difficulties we face are because the forms of our common life have, over recent centuries, become wedded to modernism. In the light of the emerging culture as outlined above, the existing structures seem remote and irrelevant, with all the sexiness of a dusty museum of religion. It may be helpful to briefly look at some of the ways in which this lack of connection with the culture is evident in church life. It's not that the old ways were wrong. They were perfectly suited to a different era. But now that the times are changing, the form of the church needs to change with it, and some people will need to lead that change.

CONFESSIONS AND DOCTRINES

Once the unity of the Western church was lost in the Reformation, people in the different camps needed to find reasons why they were right and the others were wrong. In the process, they managed to generate a great number of words in the form of confessions of faith or distinctive doctrines. The centre around which many denominations gathered was now a collection of ideas rather than an act of worship. In a climate of rationalism, the propositional and theoretical nature of the faith strengthened. Within evangelicalism particularly, there has been a tendency to imagine that following Christ involved giving assent to a set of ideas. This intellectual approach to Christianity means that it seems very dry and boring to outsiders and sometimes participants; a suspicion frequently borne out by the preaching.

AUTHORITY AND CONTROL

In the early days of the faith, the Christian community was relatively unstructured, fluid and chaotic. The associated disorder is frequently the subject of the apostle Paul's writing to such churches. It's not surprising, then, that before too long there came the desire to establish a little more order and decorum through establishing structures and clear lines of authority. These developments are inevitable in the formation of institutions to carry movements through history. Unfortunately, the trade-off has been with such things as the dynamism of the Spirit, the participation of the people and the freedom of belief. In an age when unresponsive institutions look as doomed as the dinosaurs, the church appears archaic and arthritic. And the more the surrounding culture relaxes, the more intent Christian leadership seems to be on controlling the masses through the application of authority.

D'you know that it takes 13 minutes to read the whole sermon on the mount out loud. I reckon that should be set as the universal absolute standard for sermon length. A good biblical precedent if ever I have heard one.

Huw

THE BIBLE AND ALL THAT

In uncertain times it is tempting to cast about for some rock to cling to for the sake of self-preservation. Some sectors of the church have taken refuge in Scripture, seeing it as the last bastion of absolute and revealed truth which can avoid the slippery slope into demonic chaos. There is in certain quarters a movement to try and establish 'biblical principles' in law and morality. The problem here is that we live in an age when appeals to absolute truth no longer find a ready audience. It seems to outsiders like intellectual chicanery; a ruse in order to get the upper hand. The possibility that the Bible and Christians have something to say is not ruled out. But claims to divine authority will be dismissed as irrelevant. If we are to gain any right to speak, it will need to be on the same basis as Jesus' authority: the force of our character in encounter with the world.

PEWS AND PRIESTS

People sitting in rows facing the front with the flow of conversation directed by a robed 'president' may be familiar to Christians, but the environment is strange and patronizing to many observers. Perhaps the closest analogy for many of them is that of the classroom or school assembly, which is not always a happy association. There is a problem with the cultural *form* of the church worship service. The communal singing of hymns is one example of a tradition which has become anachronistic because of the changing culture. It is not that the church should simply mimic the culture; but nor should it seek to impose cultural aberrations on people, unless we want to repeat the mistakes of jingoistic missionaries who assumed their culture was superior by definition. In a time of relationality and hunger for participation, many of the ways that things are done in the gathering of the community could be looked at again. If faith is to have any bearing on the surrounding culture, it needs to have a certain degree of resonance with that culture.

THE FORM OF RELIGION

It is difficult to do similar things over and over without their becoming familiar and losing some of the awe and meaning which they may once have held. Many of our central rituals of faith have become rather routine, so that we go through the motions without much reflection upon them. While not wanting to discount the value of ritual in preserving faith over time, there is the danger that good churchgoing folk can become practical agnostics through wooden repetition of words that no longer register in the heart. With many people outside the church spiritually interested and hungry for experience, the ecclesiastical halls can prove curiously unrewarding for them. Some Christian folk seem bemused by the concept of spirituality, and fearful of any talk of experience in relation to their faith. Church therefore becomes remote from the wider quest of the human community.

Changed Playing Field

Until relatively recent times, it was possible in the West to take a reasonable knowledge of Christianity for granted. The faith permeated and interacted with the culture at many different levels, contributing a great deal of symbolism to the imaginative environment. In the heyday of Christendom, it was psychologically more difficult to *not* identify as a Christian than to be a good Christian citizen. Nowadays the opposite is true. The plausibility structures – those commonalties accepted by a society at large which enable related claims to be meaningfully made – have almost disappeared for Christianity. To invite someone to follow Jesus in the emerging culture is akin to suggesting that the finest thing one can do for one's country is to go to war and die. The church is in a different playing field, and the old ways don't work in the same ways they used to.

All of these changes and more mean that tinkering at the edges of the church will not be sufficient to meet the challenge of this millennium. We need to start at the beginning again, and rethink the whole way we 'do' church. Not in any sense to disrespect or casually discard that which has been passed on to us by our forebears in the faith. But part of the responsibility of being stewards of that faith is to learn how to live it and declare it in our own time and setting. We live in a time of transition, and it will be uncomfortable travelling for some time to come. But God is with us, and beckons us into the new territory. The one certainty is that there is no way back to where we've come from.

What then of the future? How do we forge a way into the unknown, with nothing but a clumsy compass of the Spirit to guide us? What can be done? In this chapter, Cathy reflects on some of her own journey with Church, a community in the heart of Sydney. As they have travelled together into the unknown, they have continued to learn and grow in ways which may be helpful to others just summoning the courage to begin.

Tracking God

Once upon a Sunday morning, everybody went to church. Now, just about everyone lives outside its walls. Many of us who still frequent the establishments are only hanging in their by the strength of our fingernails. (If it were not for the incarnation of Cafe Church, I doubt that I would now be a participant in any form of Christian gathering.) Some of us have already walked beyond the walls of the institution. We may still believe in the value of meeting with other Christians, but have no idea where to go or what to do about that now …

The church can sometimes resemble a madman who is rushing to bring the harvest into his burning barn. There have been times in my life in which I have been passionately

> Sometimes I've found God hanging around in a church, and sometimes in a quiet cup of tea. God has been present in time spent with a friend, and in a piece of art, a song or a story.
>
> Jemima

involved in traditional church life. Sold out to it. I always wanted my friends to access the freedom and rest which I had found in tracking the God, but somehow bringing them to church to find such things seemed an anathema. I loved the people in my churches, but the environment seemed crumpling and smothering… especially for creative types.

At a time in my life when I felt that I had been circling the pack at a distance for long enough, I began to yearn again to be 'involved'. To do something risky again, to strain again to see what God might be doing, where the way ahead might lie. Many times in the past I had rushed in where angels fear to tread, stirred up a lot of trouble, then rushed out … usually to collapse in an exhausted heap. This time I knew that I did not want to journey alone. I wanted to stand with a group of like-minded but diverse people. And from there to walk, slowly and deliberately and prayerfully. Walk in a way which was sustainable across the land; down into gorges, up over the ridges and beyond … stumbling after the God, hoping for hope, struggling to love.

Once upon a time my idea of 'mission' was getting together with one group of people in order to 'do something to' another group of people. Our group usually bore little resemblance to the other. We might have called our endeavours 'cross-cultural'. Where one whole lot of people are IN the church, and another whole lot of people are outside the church, then there is a need for some to cross borders and learn the language of the other. In these strange days the truth is that 'everybody' is missing from the church. While people all over the joint may be seeking and exploring spirituality and finding and experiencing God, few are flocking to church to conduct that search, or feel it necessary to join in organized religion in order to live the life of faith.

How can we expect others to come to church when we don't even enjoy it, or find meaning there? If we desire to meet with others, and support each other as we try to follow the sandal-prints together, and share the puzzles of life and faith, then we must create something which we are prepared to own — meaningful for ourselves, which reflects the issues which we are facing in our lives, and which we consider has an integrity to which we are contributing.

We cannot hope to 'run a show' for others. We must seek to create a place that cuts into our own hearts and souls, where the God can stir and soothe, rend and reunite us. If we can create something which is authentic for ourselves and the people with whom we stand, then perhaps others will identify with what we have begun to build, value the opportunity to make their own contribution, and join with us in our adventure. Around the fire the travellers gather; seeking realness, safety, honesty, integrity, openness, and tough love.

Could the confusion and discomfort and yearning that is rumbling in the hearts of so many actually be the stirring of God? Could the straining towards new ways of being church together be the call of the Spirit? What have you always dreamt church could be? … Let's do it.

The Importance of Making a Start

Beginning. Now, that's the hard part. Talking, scheming, gossiping, blagging … bagging and wishing, hoping and dreaming … these come easily. There may be no end to them, unless we end them with a Beginning.

I remember the first night, opening night, at Cafe Church. The yearning for something new had begun in the people so long ago, that only a few of the tribal elders could remember and retell the story. We who remained had been meeting and scheming and praying together for a few weeks. We talked, scrounged, invited, panicked; and had finally arrived on that evening, arbitrarily designated as Opening Night. After it was over and the last of the coffee drinkers had wandered home we looked at each other and said, 'Oh no … do we have to do it all again next week?!!'

This difficulty of deciding to make a start has been exceeded only by the prospect of bringing it all to an end. Who knows when that will be, or how it could come about? The momentum since that first night has been generated by fear, God, passion, sorrow, hope, desperation, and love amongst the people who gather… the combination of these keep the creature on the move, stumbling across the land from week to week. Here we are, now part of the way across a plain of unknown breadth, seeking the Christ, cherishing community, straining towards hope and new lands.

We have begun.

Who Are We Doing It For?

In the beginning we thought we were dreaming up a new gathering for ourselves: the eight of us. We each had an ingredient or two to place in the pot. We stirred gently, and began to bring the broth to boil. We plotted an evening gathering, of informality and honesty, of art and mystery, of questions asked and meanings sought, around our friendship and the Christ, with good strong real coffee.

Passing friends sipped from the simmering spoon. Their comments shocked me. People seemed genuinely interested. More enthusiastic questions were posed than we yet had answers for. The most unlikely people in my life were heard to say, 'I could go to that … If it were crap I wouldn't go again, but I could go to that.' The responses amazed and terrified me. I began to believe that we were hitting a nerve; perhaps only just scratching the surface of something which was much bigger than we had imagined.

Even before opening night this overwhelmingly positive response posed us with problems … we began to worry about 'the numbers'. 'What if 200 people come! We won't have enough cake … We will be wasting our time if we set up for 40, and only the eight of us show up …'

The last thing I wanted on a Sunday night was to feel depressed and guilty. I did not want to begin believing that 60 people would turn up on the first night (and thereafter), when in actual fact only the eight of us seated here might be there. I suggested that we design a programme that would cater for between six and sixteen. If only we gathered, I wanted us to be glad to be together, to encourage one another's lives, to have a good night together. If more decided to value what we offered and join with us, we would need to be ready so that they could be welcomed and included.

I think we need to be fairly clear about the who. At a time when more and more of us are abandoning traditional incarnations of organized religion, can we dare to create an alternative? I believe that we must start this process by looking at ourselves; at what is really going on for us, not what we wish we could say about our life and faith. As we begin to question together, unravelling our pasts, considering our presents, and dreaming of our future, we turn the soil in preparation for the growth of something new.

Let us ask: Who will benefit? Who are we doing this all for? For whom do we dare venture into the unknown? Can we give up the idea of creating something for an imagined third person? Can we let go of the need to do something TO others? It may be a lot less nerve-wracking to arrive with the goodies and begin to merrily distribute them. A lot safer than making yourself vulnerable; safer than sharing with others from your own brokenness; safer than digging deep and revealing my own real struggles, needs, doubts and dreams …

We are together and we have our dreams. We have begun to weave our relationships beyond the fortnightly gathering time. We have begun to invite others to come and see. We have begun, and it's a relief. It gives each of us, in different ways, some of what we needed to go on being Christians in our world.

Sue

When we begin to do this we begin to stand together. When we conspire to create we begin to travel alongside one another. When we seek to make a space, a place, a time of gathering for one another, we avoid the danger of controlling the show from a position of safety, where we/I do something TO you. Let us move towards mutuality in our struggles; and form a culture of vulnerability, safety, honesty and valuing as we encourage each other along the road of life and faith.

Is being church about providing a service? If we believe this we may begin to speak about the market and the target audience. By doing something solely to and for the Other, we run the risk of being nominated for this year's 'Patronising Bastards Award'. If our role and endeavours within the group do not nurture us spiritually, then we will probably need to go looking for this elsewhere. If we fail to seek or find a context in which we can be refuelled, and instead live without sustenance for long enough, then we will either face the unpleasantness of burnout, or become that most abhorrent of Christian creatures – the saviour-come-attacker who now vents anger and aggression upon those we once served.

If we consider church the gathering of we who stumble together towards the Christ then perhaps we will engage in a form of do-it-yourself worship: growing the DIY community of faith.

As we say to those who would visit us and offer their wares, 'All we want is your heart.' I believe if we're not at least addressing and acting from our own hearts, we probably won't be meeting anyone else's either. If we can create something which we find authentic, then there is a chance that this will resonate with others also.

We at Cafe Church have endeavoured to create an experience which was meaningful and helpful for each other. We shared our lives, pointed towards the Christ, and assisted one other to follow. As others have joined us and become the people of Cafe Church, we have sought to create an environment in which any and all who gather can contribute. Contribute not only to content, but to direction.

Let us begin as we mean to continue …

Daring to Hope Again

When we were just starting out, a friend said to me that our activities were a very scary and serious business, because effectively we were 'asking people to hope again.' Daring them to hope after having suffered hurt; sometimes deep and disabling hurt.

I can remember shivering at the thought of 'ministry'. Invitations to lead on camps, join groups, or initiate programmes had never been so easy to turn down. There was absolutely no way that I was going 'out there' again. I was tired of edging my way out onto limbs, risking myself for what I believed to be true and worthwhile; only to one day look back toward the trunk and see someone perched on my branch, merrily sawing it off. No way. Not again, and not alone.

When I eventually began to dream of doing something with others, I was scared by the thought of hoping against hope. Knowing that if I began the journey of caring for others once more, I would be hooked as before; and that the risk of pain, damage, disillusionment and betrayal would once again be high. In these strange times, we are asking those who have never before darkened the doors of church to enter into something which they believe is an old and washed-up paradigm. 'Church' is considered by many to be something which was tried and has failed. Those who have made a personal attempt and have left by the back door (whether running screaming or slowly limping away) are usually no longer keen to return.

Others remain and struggle with the current form of the church. They are ready and aching for change, and know that unless something soon gives way, their weariness will slacken their grip on what little is left to them. They know that they won't be able to hang in much longer. This weariness is not necessarily all-pervasive or disabling. Some of these weary souls can muster a surprising amount of energy, once something deep and forgotten is tapped. The treasures of integrity and community, creativity and hope inspire us. Show us something we consider worthwhile and watch us work and bleed and die for its realization.

Safety, Accountability, and the Rug Treatment

When you set out to plant, consider if there is a local farmer who might consider that plot of earth to be his/her own turf. Stake out a small plot with the permission of the neighbours. Ensure that it is safe and secure, and that you cannot be run off the land next week if the weather changes.

Find witnesses and supporters outside your group who can observe and offer perspectives. Consider who might be able to stand up for you in the assembly.

and protect you in your infancy, and believe in you so that you might have a chance at longevity.

Build on a sure foundation. Be wary of depending on a rug which can be pulled from underfoot. There is a real need to protect yourselves in the early stages. This needs to be held in tension with creating lines of accountability, with feedback coming from outside your primary community. This might be represented by a group of supporters who empathize with what you are trying to do, but who may be able to offer perspectives not possible from within. Ask them to observe what you are doing, and offer advice. Inviting constructive criticism early on in the piece can head off trouble at the pass.

If you are connected to another group, or denomination, then it can be very important to have some 'friendly faces' amongst them. Find some people you can trust, and keep the lines of communication open. There have been too many groups who have suffered devastation from outside once their size and activities are successful enough to be noticed.

You will need to clear a little bit of space on the ground, so that the first shoots can begin to emerge. These first fragile offerings will need some protection … From hijacking, from destructive criticism, from insensitive trampling. The presence of any restrictions or limitations (as far as possible) should be known from the outset.

> Let's be what we want to be in the future, now. The journey itself is to be the end in itself. We need to start living the way we believe such a gathering should live. Otherwise, we sit here as a planning committee, producing a commodity to be consumed at some point in the future. I want this to be organic, and evolve as our relationships to one another in community evolve.
>
> Sue

Be careful not to try to 'poach' people from other groups. There are so many people who are already adrift from the realms of organized anything, and so many more who have never been associated with a gathering of Christians. Cannibalizing other groups creates bad blood. Let us trust God and each other, and walk gently upon the land.

Stand Alone, As-Well-As, In Parallel, Instead – Of, Either – Or

There are several ways to skin cats, so I'm told. There are several places to position your New Beginning. Among the options are:

- introducing changes to the community and gathering which is already in operation (a few new bits here and there, or a more profound undercurrent of change);

- creating a new gathering/event/community which exists in parallel to those in existence;
- deconstructing, rebuilding and replacing a current gathering with something new;
- beginning something from scratch with links to a current body;
- putting up a tent in the middle of nowhere, digging the earth, and praying that something will grow.

An attempt to transform an existing gathering can take place on a number of levels, including style, content, direction, participation, membership, leadership, *raison d'être*, etc. It is in such ventures that all the pain can arrive earliest, with short sharp shocks. It is a hard hard road, I believe. The reactions and confrontations can begin very early (most often with those who are happy with the way things are, and who resent and resist change). Sometimes, the need to preserve form conflicts with the need for change. These conflicts can cripple that which is struggling into existence. We need time to clarify our vision, to learn the ways of the new frontier.

> I am passionate about alt.worship – for me it's a lifeline in terms of church. I also feel it holds a lot of clues for the wider church and the future. It gives me a lot of hope. I'm always excited to hear of new groups getting going however frail they are.
>
> Jonny

The cry goes up: 'Why don't you run a service?!' Nice offer if you can get it, but be careful. Those who linger in the halls of organized religion and yearn for a wind of change to blow out the dust are usually yearning for something else as well. Solidarity: connection with others who share their ideas and can appreciate new forms of worship. If you are feeling alone in your struggle, then being plunged into organizing a risky experiment and making it a success can end up alienating you further. The possibility of being the focus of critique from the current unsuspecting congregation is an unattractive option. Alone and exposed and ridiculed is not a happy place to be. In your beginning, go for safety and friendly faces.

Being granted a little space to experiment with something new can be the buffer that we need in the early days. I do believe that in the end, we need to maintain and even forge some links with the people of the big church … Too many 'radical preachers' have been relegated to the back blocks by their embarrassed and annoyed denominations. The island may thrive while consuming its own produce, but in the end, with the death of key people and their passion, the island becomes exhausted, and we all try to swim back to a larger land mass. Some never make it.

I believe that resentment grows up easily between the old and the new. On the one hand, we want our children to find their own way to happiness and prosperity.

Secretly, we may desire that the path they choose be the path that we once walked. We feel proud and validated. If it is perceived that the kids are trying to 'get out and up', then we feel shamed and ridiculed. We resent their ungratefulness, their blindness to the place to which we have brought them. 'Wasn't I good enough for ya?!' I believe that it takes some long hard yards to continue to reconcile the relationship, while also moving ahead ... I believe it is possible. I believe it is as possible and as painful as the bridging of the generation gap, with love. Isn't that what we're talking about? Where each new generation inherits what the last has set up, finds it doesn't quite fit, and tries to make some adjustments?

But if the fringe dwellers are left stumbling around on the perimeters, then they will soon fall off, into oblivion; i.e. they get deleted from the ranks of the denomination. They will be replaced by others moving out to the fringes, and so on. Every preacher has seen this. Add to this old phenomenon another: people just ain't comin' in so much no more. Add water, stir, allow to stand ... hey presto ... No more people in the buildings. Somehow, we have to try to diffuse the situation ... to disarm the feeling that wanting things to be different is so unfriendly. We need to gradually build a culture which expects metamorphosis and growth with the passing of the years.

Co-existence

I am interested in co-existence. I believe that by definition an 'institution' is something which preserves itself. I am interested in creating and continuing a discourse with the big church, not because I expect her to change and follow my suit, but because I want to be neighbourly. I don't expect my mother to go get a mohawk just because I have a funny haircut. But I do want to be able to talk to her, and continue our relationship, in spite of the increasingly different external expressions of our inner worlds. (Secretly I do hope that something of what we are seeing and learning may be melded into the more traditional models, in the same way that in earlier times the discoveries from overseas mission fields influenced activities at home.) I want to continue a relationship with the big church, and hope and pray that our various visions and goals are not mutually exclusive, and that we can have the grace and skill to negotiate situations in which we can both live, with respect and love.

We need to find ways to live and gather and follow Christ alongside the Big Church. We need to find means of communicating with her. We need to find gentleness and perseverance and humility, to hear and be heard, to live and to learn, to gather and grow. Some great moments of pain in my life have occurred in the chasm between zealous, raw, naive, reckless self-giving of the passionate, and the solid, long-standing, documented expectations of the established order. When the letter of the law comes to bear on the spirit of the law it is not the general principles which annoy me, it is the result which I have seen so many times that my eyes run bloodshot with tears. I have seen the energy and the hope and the passion of the few little fragile people, drain away, choked away, gutted out of them as they buckle double with the kicks of piety and propriety.

> This is the litmus test: could we invite all our friends along to our gathering?
> If not, why not?
>
> Rupert

We need to find a way to protect the tender shoots as they emerge and grow. We need to create a clearing on the ground in a corner that gets a little sun. Somehow we need to find some space for the small fragile attempts at hope, and allow them some time to grow, before they must carry the weight of expectation and scrutiny. I think there will be many times and places where it will be impossible for the new to live and grow while in association with the old. There will be many situations in which we must put some distance between us, and draw our water from different wells. God have mercy.

So before you expose all, attempt to find others who share your dream, who struggle with similar issues, and have energy to form something new. Find others who empathize, who are feeling similarly confused, uncomfortable, lost, alone … Suggest to them the healing power of meals and talk, or more simply, plan a scrumptious meal and invite a crew over for the night.

> The duty gene is now regressive. People don't do things out of feelings of guilt and duty any more. We do things because we feel they are worthwhile – to us and to others.
>
> I don't want to go to church only because I would feel guilty if I didn't. How many rallies and 'invitation' services have you been to where only the regular churchgoers are there …? Why don't we invite our friends to come? I can't help thinking it's partly because actually we don't really enjoy it. We are embarrassed by what we do together, and know that it is far removed from the issues and needs in the lives of those around us. If we who are currently inside don't like church, then what can be its future?
>
> Anon.

Wiping the Slate Clean

I have noticed that some people have moved their churches into cafés. I have noticed that some people have hacked out the pews and brought in little tables and chairs. I have noticed that the leader may remain seated when he speaks, and the musicians may have cups of coffee next to their guitars. I have noticed that sometimes we change the way our church looks, but I wonder if we have changed the way the church actually is. Have we changed the way we are being church together or just the way we sit together?

What are some of the base premises on which our worshipping communities are built? What do we value? What informs the look that a passing participant might see/find?

Informality, intimacy, realness, safeness, the genuine, the low-tech, the casual… the lives revealed and lived together. Food drink conversations. Coffee, cake, yarning. Tears, laughter, jokes, hugs, applause. Self expression: ideas, images, sounds, voices, movement. Grace – what can it mean? What are the implications of saying that all are welcome?

In the context of meal, of friends and wine and dreams, let us wipe the slate clean of our presuppositions and begin to ask some basic questions about the gathering of the people.

New Worship, or Alt Worship, is not a package. There is nothing to buy. Nothing to take home. Hardly anything to borrow or emulate. It is the invitation to ask questions, and to struggle through and live out the answers with your people in your context. The aim is to create a means of corporately expressing our faith as part of the journey of life we have together. How can we make our worship and life together reflective of the real issues, needs and experiences in our everyday existence? And in doing so, make the road of following Christ accessible and comprehensible to those who have had no previous association with the church? How to provide a re-entry point to those who were once a part of Christian gatherings, but have moved far from their midst?

It's about asking questions, without presupposing the answers. Asking basic questions. Stripping back, rather than building up or adding on. Reflecting on what we have done in the past. Considering what we find meaningful now.

Not just asking – Do we need to make any changes to the physical environment of the church? but, 'Do we want to meet in the church building? Would another venue be more appropriate? Where … and Why …?'

Not just what songs will we sing, but, 'Do we want music? What kind? What purpose does it serve in the scheme of our overall philosophy and intention? When will it occur? What different types are available to us? Who among us has a passion for music – creating, playing, understanding, listening? What forms of music and song have the people in our group experienced before in worship?

What do they think about those forms now? What types of music do we buy and enjoy at home? What concerts/parties/events/gatherings do we attend? Do we need to use a consistent style? Can we have a variety from week to week, to create different effects? How will we respond? With dance and movement? How can we arrange the space to encourage/allow this?'

'How do we become a community, create a gathering, which is safe, real, intimate, authentic? How do we recognize our own pasts, our current issues and needs, the culture all around us, and where God is already at work in our lives?'

Asking questions about all sorts of things: when, where, why, who, how ... Should the answers we find be set in stone, or can we evolve over time, and as different people join our gathering? Philosophically, I'm convinced we should be primarily concerned with daring to ask some of the difficult questions about life and faith, and supporting one another as we struggle to discover the answers and stagger after the Christ. A lot of time can be spent trying to summarize the correct answers, distil our corporate tenets of faith, and hand them out to all and sundry. But where in the end does this take us?

There is a need to answer these questions for ourselves, for those already sitting around the table; not on behalf of some imagined third person who is out there somewhere, and who might come in ...

Manifestos

Some groups have cobbled together manifestos. While you may not be able to cover all the bases, or even agree on very many things, it can still be helpful to get something down on paper. Knowing why you are doing what you are doing is important, because it focuses you. What you do and why you do it may change with the movement of time and people, but keeping some kind of record of your hopes, aims and dreams can help you reflect on the path with its twists and turns.

We hope and pray that the emergence and life of some of these focused groups will encourage other people to create gatherings within their own sub-culture. By definition these groups are metamorphosed by the people who gather. We set a certain course together. Along the way others gravitate to us and become part of the crew. They may be attracted by any number of aspects of the community. With the inclusion of each new person comes another set of needs, passions, hopes and issues. Navigating through all of these, straining towards inclusion and growth can be tricky. Sometimes treacherous. Sometimes voices from within call for radical changes in direction. There is an inherent danger that while making these changes might make the group more effective and meaningful for some, at the same time it may alienate and neglect others. There is no easy answer to this. Is it a hijack or a good idea …?

There is plenty of room in the park for everyone to play. I think it is legitimate to state the group's current aims and invite new people to join with you in their realization. Alternately, if their passion really pulls them elsewhere then perhaps you could offer your support as they create another group with a different focus.

Valuing People

I am convinced that it is all about valuing people. If we are to value one another we will need to get to know each other; immerse ourselves in the lives of those around. My favourite method for this is a long series of meals, and sessions in cafés.

The life and vitality of the community and its gathering is dependent upon the offerings made by the people. There is no room for passive criticism. If you have an idea or an opinion it needs to be voiced to the people (formally and informally) and be coupled with creative ideas, offering an alternative way of being. I believe that we cannot stand as critics unless we are prepared to offer something of ourselves as a positive way forward. We therefore need to develop and encourage ways and means by which the people can speak and be heard.

One-Size-Fits-All

Now there's a problem: as soon as someone starts saying, 'Wouldn't it be good to do something that works for us and people like us … let's have these people as our group and do things specifically and deeply for them,' then there will immediately arise the arguments of selfishness and narrowness. 'Shouldn't the gathered people of God have both old and young represented? Where are the kids? Where are the oldies? With artists and accountants? Isn't it élitist and misleading otherwise? Isn't doing things that just suit yourselves encouraging selfishness and imbalance?'

There will be no way that we can decide what the new garment church will look like. In these days of bouillabaisse and burgers, One-Size no longer fits all, and there's no use gasping and shoving and pulling and sucking in an attempt to make everyone the same shape. The good news for today is that there can be many forms for many folks; lots of courses for more and more horses.

If each person who stumbles after the Christ clusters with others who can understand them and travel with them, and together they create something unique and authentic for their journey, and this trend permeates across the land, then perhaps we can indeed bring the love and grace of Christ to all and sundry, and we ourselves make it into the promised land.

Hotdogs and Club Sandwiches

There is a great richness in diversity, but there is also the danger of creating a culture in which the lowest common denominator rules: 'Hotdog Culture'. Where everything has to be inoffensive and acceptable to everyone, we invite irrelevance and shallowness for all. I believe that there will always be diversity within any group, no matter how similar the people may seem on the surface. The richness can be mined only in a context where diversity is valued and encouraged, where the passions of the people can be expressed with heart and soul, and where each person can be heard, and their journey valued by the group. As this richness is mined, and the honesty is opened, the group is able to become even more diverse. In the opening up of our mono-culture we discover and create and encourage multi-culture.

> There is never a week that is typical of alt.worship. That's what make's it what it is, partly, the fact that you have to come for a while to build up an overall picture. Regular church is 100% repeatable and you get the whole lot every time. Not alt. stuff … It's philosophy/ theology that counts. The out- working will always be on the move.
>
> Glen

The alternative to the hotdog might be the club sandwich. You get a little bit of everything, all packed into the one biteable experience. A bit of prayer, some songs, a look at the Bible, a chat, a cuppa: each service every week. There may be some comfort in feeling that you have gotten it all, but the satisfaction of tasting and savouring each individual ingredient is lost.

We will probably need to recognize and name the fact that any style of anything will always work better for some, and tend to exclude others. The trick lies in rotation. What goes on one week will not 'work' for everyone, but it should resonate deeply for some of those present and involved. Other weeks should strike others as significant, helpful, real … so that over blocks of time everyone in the community has been valued, and experienced connection with God and others. During a typical aftermath of Cafe Church, one person might tell me how the evening had moved them deeply, while the next person might say that it all seemed a bit hollow tonight … See you next week.

Where Are Your Mates?

More and more often, I find myself staring into the bright eyes of some dude who is telling me about how they want to start up a new group, how they want it to be different, how they want to have music/drama/words/environments that are different to typical church, and how they really want it to be able to connect with kids/generation-x/adults/parents/small furry animals …

I look at them and say, 'Do you have some mates around you who want to do this thing with you? You can't do this thing alone. That's the old model: one dude initiating and executing it all. Where are your friends/peers/fellow-travellers who can see and share your vision, and mix in the colours of their own? Do you already know the people who will attend? Do you care about them? Are they people like you, who need, desire, yearn for community and this kind of gathering?'

I am convinced that no one can do this stuff alone. Not just because it gets tiring and time-consuming and frustrating. It can be all of that and more. But because I believe that the sharing of dreams, the overlaying of visions, the interweaving of relationships, and the struggles through difference and diversity, are at the very heart of these ventures. Sometimes when we talk publicly about our people and the sort of stuff we do together, people begin to wilt before our eyes – they become tired all over at the thought. Professional ministers and youth workers say: 'it sounds like a lot of work', and 'do you do this EVERY week?!', and 'I could never offer something like that in our context.'

And they're right – no one or two people can run programmes and services and gatherings which meet the needs and dreams of every group within their congregation/people. And this is precisely the point. The difficult thing that we are suggesting they do, is to allow a variety of gatherings/events to happen within their terrain, organized and attended by the people, for the people.

Leadership

Leadership is a tricky sticky business in the context of a community where we are seeking to hear and value the positions of all. Somewhere some people will need to be offering enough of themselves to facilitate the place and space in which we all live and meet. With time and her distance there will be the need for re-evaluation, goal-setting, decisions, creation and exposition of visions. We need to deliberately and carefully set aside times for looking back on what we have done and from where we have come. Times for looking around at who we are now and the ground on which we currently stand; moments of squinting towards the horizons to see where we might go and to where the God might be travelling ...

There is the need to be WITH the people, if we are to 'take' them anywhere ...

Is it not preferable to be where a few are gathered together who love one another, than with many together who couldn't give a toss ...? Where we are acting like Christ, we are becoming people IN the community of acceptance and love.

Some basic suggestions with regard to leadership:

- Limit the length of time that one can serve in core leadership.
- Communally decide how to identify and appoint those who will offer leadership.
- Communicate the process to the wider group. Make room for participation in the process at the ground level. Regularly tell the group about the bits and pieces which are required for the group to continue its life together. Let the group know who are performing various functions, what is involved, and how they can offer support.
- Clearly state the ways in which any and all can contribute to the life of the group, e.g. at programming meetings, through feedback forms, talking to various individuals responsible for areas relating to the group ...
- Create lines of accountability.
- Report issues and decisions which relate to group life to the wider group (don't just keep all the information behind the closed doors of meeting rooms).
- Think about your terminology. The words you use speak volumes. Co-ordinator, leader, facilitator, servant, fascist, elder, person offering to attend meetings.
- Engage in action and reflection: where together you plan, then do, then reflect. Seek feedback from the wider crew. In light of what you discover, plan again, etc.

Will We Lead Love?

The nature of the inter-relationships within the leadership and inner core of the community will be what we model to the wider group. If we fail to lead in love, if we consistently create conflict, and allow distrust, dishonesty and disillusionment to grow up within us and amongst us, then this is what we will teach the people. We are dealing with the unseen. That which is in the heart will always affect that which is in the body. If we believe that our inner resentments, fears and bitterness are hidden and therefore do not affect our relationships then we are fooling ourselves. These things take their toll, not only on the people who have cast these shadows in our souls, but on everyone with whom we seek relationship.

The Dark Side

When we talk about Cafe Church and its people – the ex-churched, those who have been hurt, disillusioned, those who have wandered in the wilderness – everyone assumes that our people are cynical, twisted, angsty, depressed, angry, critical, stuck, and all that black stuff. But in fact, if anything, the opposite is true. I have been struck by the yearning, the straining towards passion, hope, guts … Some people are chomping at the bit, dying to be involved, to offer themselves in the midst of their brokenness. What we witness is vulnerability, tears, closeness, care, action, change, healing …

I do believe that the potential for darkness is there. I believe that in these strange days it is essential to create safe and patient places, where people are allowed to name and breathe out their anger, hurt, doubt and disappointment. From this place the road of hope and healing can be accessed. It would be easy to engage in a lot of mudslinging and wallowing in bitterness and anger. I think that if the team had been more interested in these things, and led with our chins, the vibe in the people would be very different. Instead, we have added ingredients slowly, stirred gently, heated gradually: sautéed lovingly. We did not skewer the beast, place it on the spit and roast it over fires, burning from a deep pit. How you cook determines what you eat.

> I feel differently about going to church now. I feel good about going. Cafe Church is the first place that I haven't felt 'categorised', or 'targeted', as single, … as a woman, … as a potential Sunday School teacher … I am a person, meeting with other people. I am not wanted or 'valued' for what I might be able to contribute, but for who I am.
>
> Allison

Many people who are now church refugees have been burnt out. As in many kinds of organizations, it is the people who are perceived as talented or gifted who are embraced into the core. Once there, there may be no end to the 'opportunities' to utilise these talents. In the context of Christian community and ministry there is a tricky tension between burying your treasure in the sand (along with your head), and bleeding it away to nothing. We need to set sustainable limits on our involvement.

As we invite some of these souls to hope again we need to recognize that although they may have much to offer our newly flourishing endeavours they may be tentative in their involvement. Ex-churchgoers may be desperate for some time and space to unpack their past, and drink in the healing of friends and beverage. If we are really interested in creating places in which people can connect or re-connect with God and his people, then we need to be prepared to let people be passengers rather than labourers.

Time, Times and Half a Time

The existence and operation of any group requires time and energy to be spent behind the scenes. We need to check that this happens at sustainable levels, and that those who offer themselves do so freely. On-ramps and off-ramps for involvement, in whatever form (participation in small groups, contribution of ideas, organisation of stuff, etc.), need to be created and made accessible to everyone. Boundaries, timeframes, and expectations need to be articulated clearly and regularly.

It takes time.

It takes time to find fellow-travellers and forge significant connections with them. It takes time to ask questions and contemplate each person's response. It takes time to prepare for corporate experiences. The gatherings themselves should be times of meeting, not just a meeting time. End-times should be open-ended (limited perhaps by the tiredness of those who will lock up). It takes time to establish trust and care amongst the people; time for us to learn how to live and work and worship together; time to find room in our hearts for each other. It takes time to create the processes which will enable our community to function and grow. It takes time to be changed by God and by each other … and change we must.

Belonging

Sometimes being welcomed into a church feels like being collared into a role. Sometimes visiting a new church can be like going for a job interview. 'Where do you come from? How long were you there? Did you know so-and-so? What was your role in that organization? Do you have experience with youth/flowers/worship/children/lawns/coins/studies/speaking/newsletters/toilets/cucumber sandwiches?' Sometimes you can get a job offer before a dinner invitation.

Is this the way we welcome people, encourage them to be involved with us, and find a place of belonging … by finding them a role? Certainly, working on a project with a group of others is great for bonding. Maybe we can begin to reform the process of inclusion by allowing people to self-select their level and way of involvement. Give people lots of ways of connecting with and contributing to the community. Give them lots of space to find their place within it. Give them time to hang about with the people already encamped, to feel the vibe, to see what already exists in the heart of the gathering. Model a community where we have time to yarn, eat, sit, laugh, be.

You can't make people belong. What is your passion? What is in your heart that you want to offer to the people? What would you like to offer … Somehow, when we find our groove, and give it all we've got, it doesn't seem like work any more. We make our small offering, the people are enriched, we feel valued, and we are drawn more deeply into the heart of the people. That's the theory, anyway …

Liking Each Other

The passion has to be for the people, above and before the 'event'. It seems to me that if these new groups which we insist on creating and resourcing are to have any kind of longevity of relationship, then we actually have to like the people who come. And like them more than just a bit, I think we have to like each other quite a lot. Of course there will always be love. We can always muster the love to talk to and care for people whom we find uncomfortable, uncommon, and unpleasant. But do we actually like spending time together? Now that we have sat near each other for a few weeks, can we be friends, have we become friends, are we offering ourselves in friendship?

Ask yourself: if the programme, the structure or the meeting collapsed tomorrow, which of these people would I continue to see? Who would remain in my life? Would they come over for dinner, drop by the house, invite me to a movie, find me in my distress? Would I miss them? I mean actually miss being with them? Who are the survivors, and who is left behind on the road when life changes her tack …?

God, you have given us love; can you enable us to be good friends as well?

Advertising Doesn't Work

Perhaps this is overstating it a wee bit. I mean, it will not do what you may hope. It will not fill the room that you have laboriously prepared with the special strangers who will make it all worthwhile. Advertising in the local newspapers, around telegraph poles, and via letterbox drops will bring no one through your doors. At least, not advertising in isolation. We make time, in a life in which we consistently say there is no time, for relationships. I miss three-quarters of the things that I 'really want to see' in this town. When I do go, to that movie/concert/exhibition/event, I go with my friends, or else they go with me. Researchers of church attendance have been saying it for years, and I'm saying it again here with regard to new and alternative gatherings and events: when we do show up, it is as a result of an interesting invitation by someone we like.

All groups have that fantastic story about that person who just rocked up because they saw a poster/flyer/line of text somewhere-or-other. But it will be one in a hundred. Not a hundred in one night. On the other hand, advertising is good because it is hip. Street-cred points can be gained by those who place funky ads in local street rags, next to posters for dance parties, exhibitions and evenings with underground personalities.

Advertising is good because it gives us 'presence'. Presence in print media, over the air waves, on the rack with the other postcards in your favourite cafés. Advertising is good because it gives your group 'exposure'. No-one will ever be able to say vaguely 'Oh yeaah … I think I've heard of it' if you have never stuck your logo/flyer/blag/name on anybody's noticeboard anywhere. (If you have no name, no logo, no distinctive look of any kind, then beg help from someone who has some literacy in visual media.)

Advertising is good because it 'reinforces' other moments of contact. If someone has been invited to come to some thing by someone they know, or even by someone who knows someone … and if they have held in their hand the flyer or postcard before, or torn a poster off a pole with that logo on it, and if they have really been meaning to check it out for a while now, and if they see an ad and the ad is good, and if they don't forget, and if that friend turns up again and they remember about it and aren't embarrassed, then that ad has acted as a positive reinforcement of behaviour. Specifically, the 'attend our gathering this week' behaviour. And then you can say that you haven't wasted your money on advertising space and wishful half-baked ideas.

Living Vicar-iously

We are trained to be consumers. Consumers and critics: the children of advertising and TV. It is so easy to sit back and criticize what we have been given. So tempting to distribute blame to those who have prevented us from having satisfying worship experiences, and who have failed to deliver to us a growing faith. What have we become? Are we now consumers of worship? Has church shopping become one long steeplechase? Have we allowed the sheep/shepherd analogy to go just a bit too far? Perhaps we long to rest. Perhaps we yearn to settle down in the shadow of a guru, secure in the knowledge that someone has finally got it 'right'. Living vicariously is living it up.

Where are the wise, where are the righteous?! To whom can we look for leadership, guidance, protection? When can we rest in the knowledge that someone knows? How long must we wait before we can lay down our defences, build a place of rest, settle and get on with our lives? Must we always struggle on? Will our torment, our questions, our search never end? We long to find the real Answer and its Keeper. Let us live vicariously forever!

> I wish kings were grand, the educated wise, the rich principled, the young innocent, and the fools wrong. I am the fool, and I feel alone. If it is the fool who sees the truth, then I see it. And I despise what I see.
>
> Anon

I have spoken to ministers – men and women of the cloth, the church, the sacred calling. I have realized how long it has been since I have heard their words and seen the world through their eyes. They speak of being prophets. They speak of saying hard things to comfortable people. They speak of unsettling lives in order to provoke mission, worship, action. They speak of frustration. How, they ask, can I make these people join me in mission? In response, I ask, how can you make them do anything?

For a long while I have been chewing on the idea that we the attenders of churches have sought to have faith vicariously through our ministers. They are the professionals in our field. When they stumble and fall our disillusionment and desire for revenge come from a deep sense of betrayal, and the undermining of our own faith. I have wondered about the employment situation. Where we, the congregation, feel that the minister is essentially our employee, our servant. We all have our own expectations about what this person is supposed to be doing. When their pursuits and attitudes diverge from these, we feel ripped off, hard done by, downright angry.

Ministers are set up as leaders. They might perceive themselves as pastors, teachers, evangelists, visionaries, administrators, managers, or anything else… What if they believe themselves to have the role of the prophetic? What if their very own job description is to say difficult things to their people which will fundamentally disturb them, unsettle them, challenge them, and expose them? Isn't it only the false prophets who tell people what they want to hear? What if they do not consider themselves paid by the congregation, but called by God, and stipended (not waged) to do whatever they see fit before God? This seems like a recipe for tears, hatred and despair. A world set to fall.

What If?

What if the congregation thought they were hiring somebody to hold their hand, and instead find that they are repeatedly being kicked in the head? What if the people believe that their work of service to God involves them giving money to the church, and being friendly to the minister while s/he acts as shepherd? What if they believe that giving money absolves them of any responsibility to feed the poor, preach to the unconverted, or any of the other proverbials?

When they get tired of being kicked in the head, suppose they stop digging in their pockets so deeply. Maybe they decide to withhold their support, to punish the one who is betraying their trust, and abusing the position as shepherd. Maybe they even stop coming to church. Maybe they feel justified in their righteous lifestyle and angry with the institution which has abused them in their piety. Now suppose that over time, this decrease in funds means that the prophet cannot be paid. Maybe there can be no job placement in this parish any more. I ask, if prophets are called to be rough on us, and most often they are persecuted by hardened people, then how on earth have we created such a dysfunctional system?

AND, what if the people believe that it is the professional Christians who do the work of faith. You know, the dirty stuff – the missions, the funerals, the visitations, the camps, the counselling sessions, and the soup kitchens. What if the ordinary Christian's duty is to believe in God, go to church, and put money in the plate so that the church can continue in service to God? Could it be that we believe that all these professionals are actually working out our salvation for us? Maybe everybody is trying to have their faith and life through everyone else. And maybe everyone believes in their bones that this is the way, that they are righteous, and that if God is going to be angry at anyone for failing, then he will be angry at the other guy for stuffing up the system.

I have sat with clergy and listened to their words about the emerging church and culture. We talked about the need for the people to begin to take responsibility for their own life and faith (corporately and individually), and to stop using the clergy as scapegoats. I wondered about the flip side: how easy will it be for the clergy to let go of their expectations (of their people and themselves), and let go of control so that the people can indeed begin to take matters into their own hands? To allow them to begin to steer and shape and form, and together find a new way ahead into what is as yet unknown. Can the clergy be free to follow Christ with 'works' that do not depend on the co-operation of the people? Can they be free to do their own thing in the world, while inviting the people to join with them if they choose? Can their life then be a source of inspiration, modelling, leadership?

Has our church life been reduced to the clergy desperately trying to drag us around, and us desperately trying to resist? That seems quite exhausting enough for all and sundry. No energy left for actually having caring relationships with people. How do we endure this? And why oh why would we ever want others to join us in this hothouse of high tension, frustrated hopes, and strained dreams?

I believe that the time has come for us to take responsibility (individually and corporately) for our own faith journey, our relationship with God and our community, and our experience of worship.

We the people need to take responsibility for creating and living our own faith journeys, the shape of our own communal life, and the experience of our worship together. Those who have traditionally been in power need to divest themselves and release their control, then step alongside the people so we can travel together.

Travelling On: Nomads and Dragons

We are on a journey from what has been to what will be. The sand shifts underfoot and is changing the shape of things all around. How far the people may have travelled, and the distance yet remaining ahead of us, I do not know. My question is this: how shall we travel from here?

In these strange days we share the landscape with travellers and pioneers from other times, who have sojourned, built and established what we have come to know. How can we co-exist? How do we live in peace? How can we find the humility, the gentleness and the perseverance needed to traverse this expanse? How can we show respect, and yet also move from their midst to new lands? Is the next destination beyond even our lifetimes?

Will we stumble as we go? Will we walk slowly with those who stagger, and wait with those who fall? Will some stay behind with the ailing, and attend the burial of the dead? Will some continue on, forming a long fragmented ant trail across the expanse? Will there be campsites along the way that some will call home? Will some be forever nomads in the land, travelling while alive, sleeping in death, witnessing the generations who follow as they camp, wait, move, build, and establish something from which their own children will one day depart…?

> Hopefully, God can be the God we hope he is and emerge us in a new place. Resurfacing, breathing, living together, communing …
>
> Lu

I ask 'Where are we now?' out of curiosity. I have no doubt that the journey is underway, and that one day our feet will tread on different earth, in a place of different norms and knowns. It is difficult to refrain from punctuating the time with the cries: 'How much longer? … Aren't we there yet?', even though it is obvious to me that we are not. I have no way of answering this question. Hindsight may write history. In the meantime, how shall we travel?

When the cartographers got to the edge of the explored world, they would print on their maps 'Beyond here there be dragons'. In some respects, we are now sailing past these markings. People may fear where we will end up; whether we are acting foolishly, stupidly, dangerously, even disobediently, by challenging the boundaries.

People may warn us that there is nothing to be found out there. I figure that if we go and return with coconuts and olive branches, then at least we will have a point of argument. Some of us will find land, go ashore, set up dwellings, and begin to forge a new life together. I believe that some of us must become traders, moving between the known worlds and the new, linking the two, telling stories, communicating hopes and dreams, wisdoms, and tales as long as the sea is wide.

I believe that as we journey we need to begin to make the maps and leave the signposts for those who will follow.

Concluding Remarks

Looking back over what I have written I see that this is nothing like what I would expect from a chapter about 'getting started'. There are no steps to follow.

All I have really managed to say is:

1. ask questions – big and small;

    Wipe the slate clean. Don't be afraid of questions broad, basic, simple or fundamental.

2. find some friends;

Think outside the square. You might find fellow-travellers in unexpected places.

3. sit down together with food and beverage;

There is something profound, valuing and vulnerable about preparing and sharing meals together. Some of my best and deepest moments of connection with others have been in the context of eating and drinking and yarning well into the night. We need to see each other and learn to value what we see if we are to undergo this journey together.

4. talk, tell stories, reveal passions, offer yourselves to each other;

Try to begin to answer some of the questions for yourselves, in your own context. Look at who you are. Listen to each other's hopes and yearnings and dreams. Tap into what each person is passionate about in life. Consider your own lives and the context in which you all swim.

5. do something together;

Do something small at first. Make it safe. Don't go public straight away. Don't worry about it being crap … Call it a prototype, an experiment. Then take a break, and when the dust has settled a little …

6. reflect on what you have done, and keep going;

Get together for some more food, and talk about what you have experienced together. Hear from every person about their response. Be gentle with each other … these are early days.

This stuff should be fun and energizing; quite unlike a board meeting. If it's not fun, stop. If you hate it, don't do it.

In light of all this, think about what you will do next …

(Document your process, and what you create together. Keep records and the resources that you create so that you could do it again at the drop of a hat.)

7. fall down and pray a lot, and laugh a lot, and weep a lot.

Then return to #1.

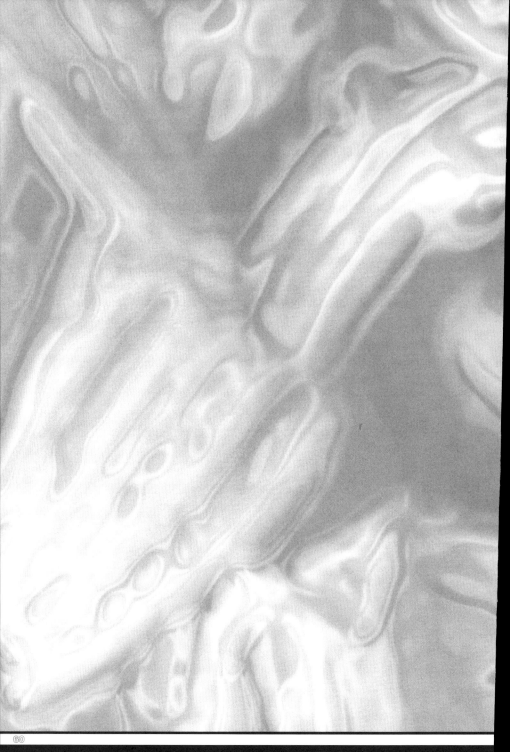

White paper leaves glowed starkly under the sole illumination of blacklight as we carried them to the beautifully sculpted wire tree and tied the ribbon to its branches. The Tree of Life bore our prayers as we knelt on one of seven cushions in a circle around a low white-gravel covered circular altar, incense drifting among us, electronic music carrying the mood. The priest intoned the words of the Great Thanksgiving, and we responded, 'Holy, Holy, Holy, the Lord God almighty, who was and is and is to come'. Bread and wine and a white stone were put in our hands. White clothing and papers glowed as they passed the blacklight. We reflected on our lives – explored or unexplored? Scripture was read. 'Unto the one who prevails I will give a white stone' (Revelation 2.17). A spoken meditation guided our private ones. We worshipped. We met with God.[1]

This took place in a large room without seating, with a bare minimum of décor – the tree, the altar and surrounding cushions – and lit only by altar candles, Five blacklight tubes and spill from two slide projectors carrying unchanging scripture texts. Two hundred and fifty people packed the space, sitting on the floor. It would have been just as moving if

> 66
>
> There are times that are so exciting it's untrue. With an amazing atmosphere and wonderful things happening. Then there are other times. Times of weeping. Times when individuals in the group are broken-hearted, times when we're all just tired for one reason or another.
>
> Sue
> 99

only six people had been present. This is new worship or alternative worship at its best.[2]

This section looks at how you could go about creating this kind of new worship and raises some of the issues that go with that territory. Are the songs of Marilyn Manson as acceptable in worship as those of John Wesley? Can pies and beer carry as much mystery and meaning as bread and wine? First, though, a look at a different way of approaching worship and worship preparation, followed by some of the characteristics of worship that should be considered if you want a different model from the mainstream/traditional one. Then the question, 'Does anything go?' in worship, and in the final section some practical ideas to help fund your journey into new worship.

Worship as Art

The entrance to the art gallery had become a dressing room. My daughter and I were each fitted with a clear plastic body suit (stapled to fit around our contours), plastic bags were tied over our shoes, surgeon's rubber gloves put on our hands, and the outfit topped off with a white hardhat with full clear visor. Looking like we were ready for a DIY tour of Chernobyl we were ushered through a décor of hanging plastic strips into a huge white space. Floor of white polythene. Wall and ceiling painted white. Large floor-to-ceiling flexible mirrors along the walls distorted our movements.

A dozen or so big circular children's paddling pools were spread around the space. Each of the pools had a fountain – spurting paint. The pools were each filled with a different coloured paint. Occasionally paint sprayed down at random intervals from shower roses hidden in the ceiling. The space and audience were splattered in paint! It was confusing – not what I expected in an art gallery – and wonderful – we were part of the installation. Participants, not just spectators.

I have no idea now what the installation was meant to be about. I don't think I did back then! Something about 'forcing a confrontation between audience anticipation and participation' according to the gallery notes. All I could think about as we slipped around the paint-splashed floor between the fountains and pools, and stood under paint drips and sprays in our child's-play version of space suits, was: 'Wouldn't it be great if we could do worship in a setting like this!' Active participation with open-ended interpretation. Room to move physically and cognitively. Creative context and content. Andy Warhol goes to church! If I could find some way of providing this kind of context and setting for theologically sound Christian worship, then maybe I'd have something that my old school friends could relate to. Maybe even a setting in which they could begin to understand something of how the gospel might be good news for them. Another journey of discovery had begun for me.

Singer Annie Lennox has been quoted as saying,

> Our society makes us out of touch with ourselves. The churches are finished; we don't have a pow-wow, a place to be emotional. The closest we have to that is a really great concert. There's an identification: the person on stage is supposed to express how they feel and the audience get it, they can weep, dance, go berserk, whatever they like. I think that's important. Singers are shamanistic in a funny sort of way.[3]

She's right. Church too easily becomes a place where you cannot be yourself; worship an activity that is imposed on you with a set response expected regardless of how you feel or what's been happening in the previous days. Worship always communicates. The problem is that much of what is communicated isn't helpful.

The more I thought about my paint pond experience, the more I began thinking about the possibilities of art as worship, and more significantly, of worship as an art. In particular, of worship preparation as an art. What would happen to the worship I prepared if I looked at it differently? What if I saw the task not as a mechanical, logical, modernist one of putting stuff in the right order so that it 'progressed' through a form to give a predetermined message with an anticipated outcome, but instead saw myself more like a curator of an art gallery? A curator who considers the space and environment as well as the content of worship and who takes these elements and puts them in a particular arrangement, considering juxtaposition, style, distance, light, shade and so on. A maker of a context for worship rather than a presenter of content. A provider of a frame inside which the elements are arranged and rearranged to convey a particular message for a particular purpose. A message that may or may not be overtly obvious, may or may not be similar to the message perceived by another worshipper.

So instead of Worship-Leader, or Worship-Planner, I become an artist, a framer, a reframer, a recontextor, a curator of worship. I provide contexts, experiences for others to participate in.

What is Worship?

My working definition of worship is very simple.

Worship is a person or persons responding to God.

(I know it doesn't cover all the bases but it provides a clear focus that I can keep in mind.) So my role as worship producer is to provide settings in which people can respond to God. In other words, where people can listen to God, meet God, hear God, sense God, and respond – heart, soul, mind, strength – to God. This is both liberating and frightening. Liberating because it opens up a whole new world of possibilities for worship (for both context and content). Frightening because it is very open-ended and non-directive.

In Chapter 2 some of the cultural mindshifts that have taken place in the latter part of the twentieth century were described. We saw that previously fundamental beliefs in progress, objectivity, rationalism, linearity, institutions, morality, truth and reality have all been seriously eroded. Christian faith no longer has a guaranteed place to stand nor a captive audience. It is one jaded voice among the barrage of voices, and unless we can understand what is at the core of that faith and find ways of connection and meaningful communication with contemporary cultural message-bearers, the Gospel message will cease to be heard. Worship is a vital ingredient in Christian mission. We need a new understanding of what worship is about and how we put it together.

I want to further suggest that worship preparation is *primarily* about providing a *context* rather than a *content*. The context being an environment in which heart, soul, mind and strength have opportunity to respond to God. This is not to deny content (although the gospel *is* primarily about a relationship rather than propositions), but to emphasize that the content can be understood in a variety of ways according to the context it's placed in. As an example, the re-enactment of Jesus' last meal with his disciples could emphasize forgiveness, community, transformation, relationship or salvation, depending on the context it is presented in. Worship has generally majored on content, with little or no appreciation for what the context is doing to that content. For example, what does it mean to talk about loving one another in a building where we sit and look at the back of each other's heads, or to listen to teaching on the priesthood of all believers and 'body ministry' when the service is led entirely from the front by elderly white males?

If the worship producer sees herself as a curator or artist, then context becomes very important. The curator of an art or museum exhibition will arrange the elements of the exhibition in a carefully thought-through context, designing for a particular effect or response, and aware that juxtaposition, distance, light, shade, colour, texture, proximity, background, temperature, space, interaction and words will all affect how people respond. So the worship curator needs to consider all these elements of context (and more) in preparing worship for others. She is providing a frame for the existing elements, a frame that conveys a particular message; a message beyond that of the individual elements. This provides a boundary within which a certain worship content or experience is provided. The same elements arranged in a different way would provide a different context and be capable of conveying a different message.

This is the scary part. Any context always allows for a variety of interpretations. Worship leaders have known this but not talked about it, and worshippers who leave the service without being able to remember the three points of the sermon have often been left feeling inadequate or 'out of touch with God' because they were unmoved by the specific content. They didn't 'get the point'. By contrast the worship curator encourages a variety of interpretations and outcomes from the worship event. As the context of worship allows for and encourages an open-endedness – the main outcome is that worshippers have met with God in some way – a variety of outcomes is not only acceptable, it is desirable. The purpose of the curator is to enable people to respond to God with all their being, and the huge range in people types, personal experiences, time on the journey of faith, learning styles, faith stages and so on, needs not only to be allowed for, but catered for.

As an artist would encourage a variety of interpretations of her art, (each equally valid) so the worship curator will encourage a variety of responses to God. In worship this is more important than ensuring a specific content is conveyed. The content is a platform, a starting point that gains meaning and relevance, and perhaps even value, when it is given a context in worship. In my view, worship is not primarily content that we accept or reject, neither is it something that is done to us or imposed on us, or even provided for us, but rather it is a context in which we interact with God in whatever ways are appropriate for us at the time. The alternative can easily be a content-laden, directed, linear and narrow approach to worship that generally appeals to a select group who can understand it and interpret it. It becomes like 'high art' – accessible only to those with the right education and training who can 'understand' what it's about.

A Risky Business

This raises questions about whether all interpretations have equal validity, and if it is possible for an interpretation to be wrong; for worshippers to 'misread' the worship. Perhaps this is where the analogy of worship as art begins to break down. It's unlikely that misunderstanding the artist's intention with a piece of art will be of any great consequence, but the same outcome in a worship setting may mean that historic Christian faith is misrepresented. The quick response to this challenge would be, 'Well what's so different to what goes on in churches every Sunday now', but that's hardly satisfactory. I think the main safeguard must be that our worship needs to be based around the biblical tradition. These stories of God's involvement with people through history and in particular of Jesus' dealings with people, are the core of Christian faith, and if we use them as the core of our worship we shouldn't wander too far from the centre (providing we are resisting the temptation to 'explain' too often what the stories mean rather than letting them speak for themselves).

Also important here is the integrity of the worship curator. She must have the skills, understandings, insights and trust required to bring parable and punter together in an appropriate as well as a meaningful way.[4] Beyond that it is a matter of trusting each other, of depending on the Spirit to lead us into truth, and the consistent-over-time retelling of the stories of Jesus to shape us. In practice the worship we provide will rarely be as open-ended and non-directive as I may have implied. As soon as the first Scripture passage is read or appears on a screen guidance is being given and a way of interpreting the context suggested. Perhaps someone needs to formulate a 'hermeneutic of context'; a reflection on the way in which the worship environment influences the interpretation of what is happening.

I go this journey with excitement and trepidation. It is easy to feel over-whelmed, and disheartened …
I believe, as many do, there is still not 'a church' for all 'peoples' of the world. Maybe there is a need for this one.

Sue

If you think that adopting the model of worship producer as artist/curator is an easy way out, think again! If our goal is to work with people to provide contexts in which we can worship God (or maybe the best we can hope for is a context in which people *may* worship God?) then we will need to be able to do much more than just shuffle songs and link them by key. we'll need a deep understanding of who's at worship – who our community is, what's going on for them individually and corporately this week. We'll need to understand something of the breadth and depth of Christian history and of the various traditions of worship. We'll need to know about the power of symbols and ritual and be able to use both wisely.

The need to know the stories of Jesus and of God's dealings with people through history is greater, not less. More skills and understanding are required than previously, not less.

I'll never forget going to Maundy Thursday (eve before Good Friday) worship at a large independent Pentecostal church a few years ago. Wonderful facilities and resources. Superb music team. Stunning publicity. Loads of multimedia equipment. I was looking forward to the experience in preparation for Good Friday, the lowest emotional point on the Christian Church's calendar. Our opening song was, 'Up from the grave he arose'. The worship leader appeared to have no idea of context. The service was all downhill from there as far as I was concerned.

During the week I wrote this I prepared a chapel service for a theological college. The theme was: God meets us in the desert experiences of life. My objective was simple: I wanted people to go away knowing in their hearts and minds that the desert experiences of life are most often where God is to be encountered. How would I do that in 45 minutes to mind-weary theological students? I had previously preached a 20-minute sermon on the subject but wanted to provide a different context for the content on this occasion. I discussed the concept with a friend and we chose to empty the chapel of all furniture, black out the windows and line the floor with black polythene. Two tonnes of sand was trucked in and spread over the floor, candles in paper bags set up around the walls and eerie desert-wind sound effects played through the sound system.

People took off their shoes and socks and stood or sat in the 'desert'. The service consisted of four Bible stories of desert experiences, each followed by silence, a repeated acapella solo and a one-minute 'rant'. As punters left they took phials filled with sand as ongoing reminders of the experience. I'm convinced that those who participated will remember the theme of that service for a very long time. It took place because the service was approached not from the perspective of, 'what can we do to fill the time?' but from the 'worship planner as curator' model which looked at what we hoped the worshippers might encounter and worked towards that.

Approaching worship preparation as an art is risky. There is the risk of failure, of being misunderstood, of being labelled 'trendy' or 'new age', or 'not Christian', or 'lacking in content'. If you've read this far you're probably already familiar with that territory. There's also the risk that you and your friends might end up with worship that enables you to encounter God in a way you haven't for a very long time. As I said, it's a risky venture, worship.

My hope is that the perspective I have offered will provide such a contrasting way of thinking about worship preparation that you will be able to reflect critically on your own experiences and determine a way forward that best suits you and those you seek to worship with. I don't wish to trash other approaches to worship, rather to provide a new perspective for those who have tried other forms and found them unsuitable.

Arts and Minds

Before moving on to look at some of the practical implications of changing our practice, I want to introduce you to a way of reading about art that can fund your understanding of *worship* as well. Here's a recent quote from the art critic in my local paper.[5]

> Much modern art is not specific. Everything is ambiguous and has many levels of reference. As art becomes less specific it becomes more abstract.

If you replace 'art' with 'worship' it becomes an interesting statement about worship. You may not agree with it, but it provides some stimulation to thinking outside the usual 'worship box'. The article continues … (you make the changes)

> Abstract art does not exclude symbolism and metaphor but the metaphor is not specific. The artist leaves it open so that the viewers can bring their own imagination to the work and make of it what they will.

Similarly an article on curatorship can contribute to our thinking about worship and worship spaces.

> The job description (of curator) has not only been expanded, but now encompasses multiple models. The curator as producer, as team leader, as search engine, as poser of questions.

> Several salient points define the new curatorial rhetoric: an emphasis on globalisation, interaction and an open-ended, team style of curating.

> The theory issue … is how to juxtapose works from different cultural traditions in a way that respects and engages with the original context of each. In other words, how to avoid… 'presenting art from other places as if other places are all the same.' Or as if art from other places inevitably offered up a mirror image of the familiar.

> … curators have tried to transform and 'relax' (the museum's) traditionally austere atmosphere by such gimmicky means as chill-out rooms, ambient sound tracks and home-cooking in the galleries. This literal approach to humanising the museum, to imbuing it with a comfortable domesticity, seems radically naïve. If people simply wanted to feel at

home, they'd stay at home; presumably they visit a museum when they want to engage with art, and such tokenistic gestures do little to enhance and expand their possible relationships with the art on display.[6]

One final quote, from an author writing for a primarily Christian audience, about postmodern culture·

> Art always brings abstract philosophies down to earth. Artists express their beliefs in concrete forms, thus making clear the implications of their world view and dramatising what it means for human life.[7]

You don't have to agree with all these quotes as they relate to worship (or art), but they can promote very helpful discussion and thinking about worship by raising issues that otherwise might not get thought of. The world of the arts has much to say that can inform and fund the 'worship producer as curator' model.

Getting It Together

When it comes to getting together to 'do worship' in a new way, whether it be with a few friends, or a sizeable group, there are some important concepts to keep in mind if you want to avoid becoming that which you have moved away from. One of the most significant characteristics of the emerging culture is the desire for hands-on participation, at all levels. Not the kind of youth service participation where the youth leader puts the service together and then invites participants to do one of the bits he or she has prepared, but rather participation and ownership of the worship event because it is 'our' worship. I believe that worship should be firmly rooted in the lifestyles, hopes, dreams, music, rituals, fears and aspirations of the people who are worshipping. It should reflect who they are. As Cathy noted in 'New Beginnings', the moment we try to 'do worship' for a mythical third person who may walk in off the street at any moment we have lost the plot and are doomed to enduring mediocre worship that satisfies no one. Participation and involvement are first principles. This doesn't mean that everyone has to agree on every aspect of every service. It does mean that generally the worship relates to the subculture of those who are worshipping, and that at least from time to time everyone involved is able to make specific connection at depth.

The role of the producer, according to musician, artist and videographer Brian Eno, is somewhere between that of the dictator and the mediator.

> Usually what people are practising is not democracy, but cowardice and good manners. Nobody wants to step on so-and-so's toes, so nobody wants to say anything. The valuable

idea of democracy is that if there are five people in a room and one of them feels very strongly about something, you can trust that the strength of their feelings indicates that there is something behind it. My feeling about a good democratic relationship is the notion that it's a shifting leadership. It's not: 'we all lead together all the time.' It's: 'we all have sufficient trust in one another to believe that if someone feels strongly then we let them lead for that period of time.' And this is what typically happens: somebody will say: 'no, I really think we should do it this way' and I'll say: 'OK, let's try it, let's see what happens.[8]

Worship must be culturally relevant. This participation is what gives worship authenticity and builds community. It makes worship accessible by rejecting the cultural accretions the Gospel has picked up over time and allowing the heart of the Gospel to connect with the reality of life for the worshippers.

The first thing to realise is that worship is not a means to evangelism. It is not something Christians do in order that some good, however it is defined, will happen to other people. Worship is our way to God and at the same time our celebration of the love of God. The key to authentic worship is the presence of authentic worshippers. They transform the most routine liturgies into encounters with the love and glory of God. So our question is not how to make worship more appealing to people outside of the churches in order to attract them to our midst. The question is how Christians worship together authentically. If we do, we can be assured that our partners and friends may also experience God in some way in and through our service of worship.[9]

Writing about the American Church Sally Morgenthaler agrees, 'our failure to impact contemporary culture (with the gospel) is not because we have not been relevant enough, but because we have not been real enough'.[10] Perhaps you've experienced that for yourself.

A commitment to real participation also means that the worship will not be led by a single figurehead, either in preparation or in production. Leadership will move around the group and the space. The 'front' may be as difficult to determine as the leader.

Everything is considered for possible use in new worship. Nothing is too old or too new, too traditional or too postmodern, too secular or too sacred to be considered for the mix. The only elements rejected will be those that don't help achieve the ultimate goals of bringing together experience and understanding; materials and methods that promote a body/mind/soul split; themes that aren't aware of our relationship to the earth, and those exclusive in language or acceptance.

There may be little obvious logical progression to the worship. Multimedia images may be juxtaposed with ancient chants and techno music. Or even concurrent with them. The worship arises from within a local community of people who know what they relate to in music, ritual, image and symbol, and who know how far they can go with those elements and still connect the gospel with their lives. They realize they're not perfect and they expect to evolve and change as time goes by, and as God works within their lives and their community. But they are also accepting and tolerant of groups who choose to worship differently, even strikingly differently, to them. They just ask for this same tolerance to be extended to them.

New worship groups will be as concerned about creating a space for worship as they will about creating the worship. The space will reflect who they are and what they hope for from their worship. It may be a lounge or a bar, a hall or a mall, a church or a nightclub. Wherever, it will almost certainly involve the creative contribution of artists making it 'our space'. Visually attractive. Recognizing and honouring the contributions of creative people. Looking for ways to involve all the senses in worship, and to help the body contribute to the worship experience rather than fight against it. Providing opportunity for a variety of responses, and always expecting God's Spirit to turn up and being constantly surprised when she does.

> As we near the end of the millennium … I think we are back to what is called 'square one'. We may timidly admit that we are living in 'apostolic times', in times where the cloth is being woven. A risky time in apostolic mission, where we have to tell one another the basis of our hope, join with each other in the expression of the strength of our faith, telling one another the questions we have in order to find together the answers, that the world, the people, are expecting from us as disciples of Christ.[11]

Two Movies and a Story

In the much-used-for-evangelism movie *Jesus* we see a late twentieth-century actor dressed to look like the traditional image of a first-century Jesus, walking around in late twentieth-century Palestine made to look like first-century Palestine. Jesus' dialogue is that of the New Testament, NIV version. 'Our emphasis is on a Christ who never opens his mouth without speaking the words of the Scriptures,' says the advertising on my copy of the video. '*Jesus* was filmed entirely on location in the Holy Land … precisely where, twenty centuries ago, the original events took place. More than 5,000 extras were employed, all dressed in costumes woven and dyed to strict historical specifications,' it continues.

Contrast that with the Dennis Arcand movie *Jesus of Montreal*. Here is a modern story of actors employed to perform an Easter pageant. The pageant itself is done in first-century style but the story around it involves the contemporary lives of the actors. Despite it not attempting to tell 'The Jesus Story' it tellingly portrays many aspects of Jesus' life in profound ways that have stuck with me. When Daniel, the actor who plays the part of Jesus in the pageant, goes with a woman friend and fellow actor to an audition for a television beer ad, she is asked by the director to 'show her titties'. Daniel responds by imploring her not to, telling her she is more valuable as a person than the act would make her. Daniel then sets about overturning TV monitors, tables and cameras in a scene that can't help but remind the Christian viewer of the biblical Jesus turning over the moneylenders' tables in the temple. This approach to film-making takes an entirely different approach to retelling events.

Or listen to this story:

> Although only a poor peasant farmer he was considered very well off, because he owned a horse which he could use for ploughing and for transport. One day his horse ran away. All his neighbours commiserated with him and exclaimed how terrible this was, but the farmer simply replied, 'Perhaps.'

> A few days later the horse returned and brought two wild horses with it. The neighbours all rejoiced at this great good fortune, but the farmer just said 'Perhaps'.

> The next day the farmer's son tried to ride one of the wild horses; the horse threw him and he broke his leg as he hit the ground. The neighbours all offered their sympathy for his misfortune, but the farmer again said, 'Perhaps'.

> A few days later Government soldiers came to the village to take young men for the army. They rejected the farmer's son because of his broken leg. When the neighbours told him how lucky he was, the farmer replied, 'Perhaps'.

The farmer and his horses, jokes, television sitcoms, the scene from *Jesus of Montreal*, are all examples of what is known as reframing – recognising that the meaning of an event depends on the frame or context in which it is perceived. Reframing is a neuro linguistic programming (NLP) technique used in counselling situations and I'm indebted to Michael Frost for introducing me to the term in his book *Jesus the Fool*.[12] We could call it contextualizing, but reframing better describes what we do in the process. We change the meaning of an event by giving the event a different frame or context. Having a second horse is seen as a good thing – until you look at it in the context of it causing a broken leg. Reframing is one of the basic tools in the worship curator's toolbox. It's also one of the most used, the most easily misused and abused, and undoubtedly the one most likely to get you into trouble and to cause you to have to defend what you've done!

Jesus was a reframer. So was Paul. The most obvious example from each is Jesus taking the common elements of a meal – bread and wine – and giving them a very different significance; and Paul picking out a pagan statue dedicated 'to an unknown god' and using it as the text for his message about Jesus. Reframing. As we move into the third millennium in Western cultures increasingly uninterested in what the church has to say, and with people deserting churches in their tens of thousands every week, there is a desperate need for people who can make sound connections between the common ground of people's lives and the gospel story. As John Drane said at the recent British Anglican conference to signal the end of the Decade of Evangelism, "We often say that if we could only get people into the church they would realise that what it has to offer is good news. But it is the people who know us best, from the inside who are rejecting us. If we could merely hold onto our own children, who desert the church in droves, the decline would be turned around."[13] If there ever was a time when we needed to be able to reframe the church experience for a generation, it is now. Even those on the inside, with all the clues explained, aren't finding the experience meaningful or helpful.

Reframing will be at the heart of any worship experiences we curate.

Some Illustrations

Here are some illustrations of reframing, mostly based around the comparatively common ground of the Lord's Supper (although I realize that as a Baptist I have a certain lack of constraints not always available to those of other traditions).

Are bread and wine the only elements acceptable for communion? If so what bread – unleavened? white? wholemeal? cheese top? fruit loaf? – and what wine – red? white? still? sparkling? Port? Sherry? – in what volumes – thimbles full or a decent gulp from a goblet? – and what alcoholic content? In services I've been involved with we've variously used hamburger buns and large bottles of coke in a festival setting; a 'French bread stick' and bottle of wine passed around a small group until all was consumed; and New Zealand Chardonnay and Pavlova (a sweet eggs and sugar dessert) during services with a New Zealand theme. At another service where we explored the biblical story of the feeding of the five thousand we used cans of DB (the local beer) and meat pies as the items the boy had in his bag at the barbecue. Following the blessing of the items copious quantities of pies and beer 'miraculously' appeared from beneath each table in the worship space. Even more miraculous was the large quantity of beer and pies we had left over at the end of the service!

Mostly the communion has been deliberate and overt, but at times we've just had waiters and waitresses dressed in white and black carry baskets of bread and bottles of wine around the tables offering them to people after the service. 'Is this communion?' was a common question from punters as they took bread and wine. This is a question we could ask of reframing the communion. Is it communion without a conscious act of remembrance? Is it acceptable to reframe that which has already been reframed? To what extent can the second reframing depart from the initial one. At what point does reframing become distortion? What about mystery and sacrament? Can they be carried in familiar yet unfamiliar elements? Good questions. I have answers that I can live with. You will need to work out where you sit on these issues! Much of your perspective and practice will be determined by the experiences you and your fellow worshippers have had.

Ambiguity

There are more practical warnings to heed. A recent attempt to be more multi-sensory and add smell to the communion had a breadmaker on the communion table, with the timer carefully set to finish baking the bread at the appropriate time. After an initial hiccup the timing was perfect. The beeper sounded just as the communion prayer ended. What I hadn't allowed for was the heat of newly baked bread. So as I held the loaf up and dug my thumbs into it in the dramatic gesture of breaking it, the words of institution rang out, 'This is my body given for you … ouch! It's hot!' Reframing does have its dangers. A few centuries ago a French Orthodox priest was excommunicated for using pine needles instead of palm fronds on Palm Sunday. As Graham Cray, Principal of Ridley Hall, Cambridge, said,

> This is a mission exercise to a culture that's in transition, it's full of risk, full of experiment, full of mistakes, full of other Christians not liking it and thinking you're selling the Parson, that the gospel has been undermined and so on. If you want to be popular in the traditional church don't get into this stuff. It's not a comfortable place to be.[14]

There are few hard-and-fast rules when it comes to reframing, but there are some important things to be aware of. It's not done to be trendy, to shock, for novelty, for the sake of change, to show how much more you know that the rest of your group. The purpose of reframing is to make stronger, clearer, deeper, more meaningful connections between people's lives and the gospel story. Secondly, reframing requires that you understand the essence and heart of the truth you're reframing. If you have no idea what Good Friday is about, you'll happily sing 'Up from the grave he arose' on that day; if you don't understand what the Last Supper is about, you won't be able to help others to connect with God in that experience regardless of what elements you use.

Here's a story that takes those connections into consideration.

It could have been a soul-destroying discovery, yet I was buzzing from head to toe when I came down to the cafe after Community night. We had burnt Chinese money with prayers on it as it was Chinese New Year and the summer solstice. We burned up our collective wishes for God's movement in our neighbourhood.

And there on the pavement were some of my cafe workers and others from the street, with incense, and you guessed it, Chinese money scattered everywhere. They were writing wishes and prayers and setting fire to them as they offered them up for each other. Celebrating the New Year, and hope for better times. Call it syncretism or call it God's grace transforming (so called) pagan festivals into places and festivities of significant spiritual meaning. My staff did church without me, my head said, yet my heart was drowning in pride, excited at their excitement and festivness. Excited by their hope and belief. Excited at the possibilities of the journey that lay ahead for us …[15]

Recently I was involved in an email discussion about whether it was appropriate to use crystals (the New Age store kind) placed on the floor in the shape of a cross as part of Christian worship. Would you? Having agreed that the crystals have of themselves no intrinsic power, the question then depends on the worshipping community that you are part of. This is the third consideration. You need to know how your community may react to your reframing. Will they be so offended that they don't get past the crystals? Are they mostly ex New Agers for whom crystals will have levels of meaning that you're not aware of and which would be unhelpful in the context? Or is the group able to redeem these as helpful symbols in this context? Worship should arise out of a local community and what is appropriate in one context may be totally inappropriate in another. Sometimes reframing will work only if it is introduced properly, with some explanation. If the explanation has to be more than minimal then what you want to do is probably not going to be appropriate! Worship is to enable people to encounter God within the context of their own subcultural sign/symbol posts and if no one gets past the fact you have New Age crystals laid out on the floor, you've failed.

I took part in a worship service that had road kill (dead opossums and ferrets) on the floor, and where we 'anointed' each other on the forehead with used engine oil. For the rural farming community people who prepared the worship this was entirely appropriate (as were the country and western style songs we sang!). In an urban setting the effect could have been quite different.

Music, film, video, photographs, posters, paintings, sculptures, actions, rituals, images and icons of all kinds may be appropriate for reframing. Does 'anything go'? I think so. At least everything can be considered and nothing rejected out of hand until you consider the issues raised above.

Making a Start

You can't find a church that you want to be part of, so you decide to get some friends together to do worship. Where do you start?

It's important not to think big, or to think about any of the institutional models and patterns you've experienced in the past. Start with who *you* are and work at growing a pattern of worship that is meaningful and authentic to you. So it's blank-page time. Everything is up for grabs – who, where, when, how, even why.

A good way to start is to get two or three friends together who feel similarly to you. Meet in your lounge or some neutral, and probably not too public, space. You might follow a sequence like this.[16] First give out some magazines or newspapers and find three pictures between you of anything that grabs you, even if you don't know why. Decide on a piece of music to play while you look at the pictures. What track rings bells for you? Don't fall into the trap of thinking that you need to find a track that illustrates the pictures, for example Sinead O'Connor's 'This Is To Mother You' to go with pictures of mothers and children. Choosing is fairly intuitive. You might select one track for all three pictures, or a different track for each picture. Find a Bible reading that connects in some way with the music and the picture or pictures. (You could decide to use the Scripture as your starting point before you choose pictures) Finally choose a position. For example kneeling, lying, holding hands.

Now run through the sequence – hand around the picture while you play the music and take up the position. Read the Scripture. When it's over talk to each other about how it went. Was it any good? What worked well? What didn't? This is very important. Either you decide it was lousy and move on (don't give up, have another try another day) or the lights go on and you meet with God. As you get more confident with this process you can add elements such as ending with a ritual action, setting up the environment with candles or projected images or whatever.

Making Room for God

My goal in preparing worship is always to provide an experience that gives room for God to speak to those present and for them to respond to God – heart, soul, mind and strength. I keep that in mind as I curate the elements of a service and constantly question how any of the elements and their combinations contribute to that end. Good worship connects the lives of the worshippers with the life of God. "We're here to seek and to be sought by God", is a fitting call to worship.

Although I have I have long since lost track of the source of this quote it expresses rather well the participation and integration that is vital to good worship.

> 'Life is neither the candle nor the wick, but the burning'
> Even so is worship neither
> the gathering of the people present
> nor what they say and do,
> but the sharing of an experience
> of the presence of God,
> and a celebration of that experience.

If you're working on worship with a larger group – say 15 or more – you could use a process that we've often used. Divide the group into seven subgroups and assign one part of the running order to each subgroup.

1. Call to worship – bring us in, prepare for worship
2. Prayer of confession and words of forgiveness
3. Celebration – of God, of life
4. The Word
5. Responding to the Word
6. Prayers for others
7. Blessing to send us out

Decide on a Scripture text and give the groups 30–45 minutes to come up with their 2–3-minute segment. We usually do this at the end of our intensive courses that have included a variety of techniques in using video, making slides, etc., and so restrict the groups to using the overhead projector or slide projector only. No video and no music. The service progresses without announcement and we play a track of music of our choosing behind it all, e.g. Peter Gabriel's 'The Passion' or Sue Wallace's 'Prayers for the Digital Orthodox'[17], raising and lowering the volume as necessary.

I am constantly amazed by the creative responses groups come up with under the pressure of these tight parameters. Once we stood in a circle while a large wooden cross was laid on the floor in the centre. As an act of confession we were asked to turn our backs on the cross while words were spoken that picked up the things we might have done that this movement symbolised. Then as we stood in silence someone came and stood behind us one at a time and said 'Christ has forgiven you, turn toward home' and grasping both shoulders gently turned us back toward the centre, each other, and the cross. Stunning stuff. For the celebration we lay on the floor with our head on the stomach of the person next to us and had a communal laugh. The Word was chanted over a body percussion created by drumming on our knees and slapping our thighs. Simple, creative, very memorable and moving. '… the sharing of an experience of the presence of God, and a celebration of that experience'. It's called worship.

You need to start with a clean slate, a group of like-minded people. (Who wants to face criticism or have to justify what you do at this stage of the process?) This is worship for the group gathered, and no one else. And you need to take a risk.

Room for All

This might be as far as you go, getting together from time to time to worship. If your group attracts more like-minded pilgrims, or if you have a much larger group to begin with, you will need to constantly battle against the slide toward institutionalism – becoming what you have left behind. Two major contributors to that slide will be trying to please everyone every time you meet, and the pressure to keep up the 'programme' even when most of the group no longer want it, or have moved in a different direction. The influence of these factors will depend greatly on whether the worship you are running is an independent group or attached to an existing church structure in some way. The spectrum ranges from two or three friends getting together in their lounge and 'doing worship', through groups who do a monthly or bimonthly 'alt.worship' service as part of the programme of their church, to those groups that function as ongoing Christian communities i.e. churches, while exhibiting most of the characteristics of alt.worship. The middle group is the most common and the latter quite rare. So what makes these services and groups different to the mainstream church that their participants have moved away from?[18]

Some of the underlying principles at work in these groups and in most groups who describe themselves as doing 'alt.worship' or 'new worship' would be a commitment to the following.[19]

Participation: People are encouraged, but not forced, to participate in the worship. The worship event provides numerous points and ways for people to be involved, with their body, mind and emotions. The desire for hands-on participation is one of the most significant characteristics of the emerging culture. This need goes beyond 'getting Mary to read a prayer' and means involvement in the planning and preparing of the worship at all stages and levels. This is worship of the people by the people for the people. There is a high level of ownership by those worshipping.

Community Based: This relates to participation but reminds us that worship should be firmly anchored in the lives of the worshipping group. It is not imposed on the group by any outside force but grows up from within the life of that community, expresses who they are and builds them up. So worship is prepared with the needs of the community who will worship in mind. As mentioned earlier, the moment you try to do worship for a mythical third person who may walk in off the street at any time, you have lost your way. I don't know what sort of music church worship leader Tommy Walker produces but the sentiment he expresses is right on. 'People are constantly coming to me and asking, "How do you do this hip music?" … I'm not doing hip music because it's hip. I'm doing it because that's how I worship God.'[20] Worship must reflect who you are and connect with who you are if it is ever going to be authentic and meaningful for anyone else.

This call to worship expresses it very aptly …

God is here. His Spirit is with us. This is not a performance. This is our worship. This is not a rave or a disco. This is our worship. This is not a special event for young people. This is our worship. We invite each other to use the environment, the visuals, the music, and the words, to stimulate our thoughts and draw our hearts to wonder at the goodness of God. Invite God to meet us as we seek to meet God. This is our worship. God is here.[21]

Culturally Relevant: Worship will reflect the culture or subculture of the worshippers. It will reject cultural barriers that are not part of the gospel. The motifs and symbols, music and language will be meaningful to those worshipping. They may not be as meaningful for, or understood by, those outside the subculture.

No Prima Donnas: The service usually moves through without any particular leader being obvious. Elements of worship flow from one to another without announcement and people involved in leading segments will do so from various places around the space. It doesn't all happen at the front.

Wholeness: Worship will involve the whole person. Body, soul, mind and spirit. Deliberate efforts will be made to engage the whole person in the worship. Related to this is the belief that both understanding *and* experience are essential in worship, and opportunities will be created for both.

Eclectic: All of life and history and experience is in the grab bag of elements that may be used in worship. Any source of ideas, music, words, images, is considered from any religious or non-religious tradition. The alt.worship curator and worshipper reject any notion of a split between sacred and secular. They are willing to use ideas, materials and forms from the secular world in worship.

> We're sensing a longing for the old and the familiar even as time hurtles on the threshold of a new millennium. That's why we need AncientFuture Faith. Faith that's filled with new-old thinking, that re-appropriates the traditional into contemporary, faith that mingles the old-fashioned with the newfangled, faith that understands the times in which we live in order to claim the era in which God has placed us for Jesus Christ.[22]

Sweet's coining of the term AncientFuture Faith sums up the eclecticism of new worship well.

Multimedia: All forms of media are available to be used in worship – to communicate and to create atmosphere. Not only technological media like slide and video projectors but also all forms of the arts – visual, fine, performing. Use of media may not be linear or discrete. Non-linearity and concurrency are common, as is juxtaposition of otherwise unrelated items. So two readers may be alternately reading the verses of a Psalm at the same time as unrelated video images and slide texts are projected onto screens around four walls and a drum'n'bass track is played in the background. The whole is more than the sum of the parts.

Provisional: No one involved in alt.worship or new worship experiences thinks they have arrived. One of the given understandings is that we're on a journey from the modern to … who knows what? We are living in the interim between the 'then' and the 'not yet'. This is one of the reasons that worship experimentation is so vital. The 'not yet' will be shaped by the trials and experiments going on now. Anything we do is provisional, open to further change and evolution. The need for constant experimentation has never been greater.

At the same time there is no sense of exclusivity. New worshippers need to be marked by their tolerance of other forms of worship, recognizing that they are valid for other people and subcultures.

These are some of the broad principles that will shape your journey into new worship. Now for some of the specifics.

SOME OF THE STUFF OF WORSHIP ...

Creating an Environment for Worship

The most neglected and yet arguably the most important element of worship is the space itself: the room, the building. It is much more than just a neutral area in which something happens. No space is neutral. Every space impacts in some way on every person who enters it.

> All Christians (even those whose dogmatic formulations tell them otherwise!) are fully aware in daily life of the power of sacramental signs. Exactly why the bunch of flowers should nearly always do the trick, why we can almost hear them speak the words 'I am sorry' or 'I love you', is a total mystery, but it works. Our places of assembly must never become no-go areas for the working out of this universal truth. Art, design, layout, movement, clothing and gesture will all be redolent of powerful meaning quite beyond the delineation of their external attributes. We must recognise this quality in the layout and design of our sacred spaces, and use it to the full.[23]

While we may be able to do little about the structural design of the spaces we meet in to worship, we are able to affect their interiors.

The space is a vital factor of context for worship. Traditionally our worship has divided the space into two sections – the congregation, and the platform, 'up-front'; the latter being where the action generally takes place and the former where that action is best observed. Even traditions that are known for their 'participation' of the congregation in worship in fact rarely deviate from this two-way split. Church buildings reflect this understanding of worship. They are generally rectangular, with the platform at one end or side. Open/clear spaces are often minimal (except for the platform), thus enforcing the understanding that most of the action takes place at the front, and those seated are primarily spectators.

This is not how it has always been. Limited New Testament references to Christian worship services indicate that worship took place in people's homes.

We could assume that this would, at very least, encourage much more interaction between people than pew-sitting does.

According to writer Doug Adams, the early church followed the worship setting of typical Jewish worship …

> The room would be set up with a few benches along the walls (reserved for the elderly and infirm) with all the rest of the people expected to stand, move, kneel, and prostrate themselves in response to the ongoing liturgy. The minister reads the Scripture in the midst of the people: and he gives the sermon from a seated posture with people moving in closer to hear him if necessary … For most prayers the Biblical stance in worship is to stand with arms and hands raised above the head … While prayers of confession were often done in a posture of prostration, or less common position of kneeling, most other prayers of praise, thanksgiving and intercession were done in the standing position with arms raised – a posture that most opens the lungs and body … Somewhat similarly, all the people stood when the Gospel was read – a position that increases attention to the Word and indicates that the Word is to invoke action is us. The people would clap along during the singing of hymns and even applaud at the end of the minister's sermons.[24]

So involvement, direct response and movement, using the whole body and all the worship space, was the norm. The openness of the space allowed this to happen.

Time and Change

As time passed and church life became more institutionalized, the worship space took on a set form. In the East buildings were often built in the squarish shape of the Greek cross, and in the West, by the medieval era, were patterned on the elongated cruciform shape representing Christ on the cross. Worship followed the pattern of the buildings. Processionals and enactments were viewed from near in Eastern churches or from afar in the West, by passive congregations. The distancing of clergy from the congregation has been described as the architecture of ceremony and power. What is important about architecture is not the variation in decorative detail but way in which the changing shape of spaces enables or prohibits movement and interaction between laity and between clergy and laity.

The social upheaval of the first half of the twentieth-century brought a more egalitarian mood among people in many Western countries, and further architectural change. No longer was the clergy person seen as spiritually and intellectually superior. Laity were in many cases able to carry out what were previously considered 'priestly functions'. This was a move to the architecture of participation and equality and is represented by the 'fan-shaped' technology-filled auditorium. Its purpose is to maximize communication (at least aurally and visually!) and the sense of involvement (if not *actual* involvement). So we have shortened sight lines (perhaps aided by tiered seating) giving clear views of the platform and a reduced sense of remoteness from the action. This is often seen in a church turning its seating 'sideways'. While reducing the level of 'back of head' fellowship, I would argue that in fact little real change has taken place in the theology or philosophy of worship. The action is generally still at the front and led by a special group while the majority observe, albeit from more comfortable and closer positions than previously.[25]

A further development in recent times has been the move to individual, movable seating. This is said to increase 'fellowship' and allow for movement, wider aisles, and even to clearing the space of chairs entirely. Very recently larger spaces have been cleared at the front of some auditoriums to allow 'ministry' to take place. Again, little real change in theology or understanding of worship has happened despite these physical changes.

The Significance of Space

This architectural progression reminds us that the space influences what we do and how we do it. Spaces can be distancing or involving, adding to isolation or to intimacy and participation. To achieve a space that works for you and not against you it may be necessary to create a space within a space by using hanging drapes or banners or moving furniture. A large-volume space can be awe-inspiring or intimidating. Small spaces can be intimate or claustrophobic. Uncluttered minimalist spaces can be boring or meditative; busy spaces stimulating or distracting. Either way, you ignore the space at your peril. By thinking about the effect it may have on your punters you are less likely to have the space giving a different message from the rest of your service.

Whatever the shape of your worship space people need to be able to see what is going on. In a larger space this could be achieved by projecting the images onto a second screen at the side rather than having everything happen at the front. It is easier to make a large space seem smaller than it is to do the opposite. A central low platform or a central hung screen brings the focus into the centre and away from the edges. In a small space the best you can do may be to use a minimalist approach and to get any equipment you are using up off the floor leaving clean lines. At Cityside we do our Easter Art Installation in a relatively small space that is long, narrow and high. We overcome some of these limitations by removing all the furniture from the space and lining the walls to 3 metres high with black polythene against which the art is spot-lit. A central wall of polythene 2 metres high divides the space longways and promotes a natural movement around it. At other times we project images onto the ceiling making the space seem larger than it is. Coloured lights in the corners push the space out to its limits.

Avoiding the creation of a 'front' in the space encourages fuller use of the available area. Elements of worship can be led from around the space. Treat the whole space as your platform. Use a variety of places for entrances and exits. Having a voice come from behind can encourage movement by people to look at the speaker (let people know this is acceptable). Processions don't always have to be from the back to front. They can be around. People have to be re-educated to not come into the worship space and all sit facing the same way. Newcomers always look for a 'front', sometimes with great consternation when it's not immediately obvious! Generally in their search for the comfort and predictability that punters usually associate with being in church they'll make the largest screen or the one with moving images on it the front. Part of your job is to let them know that looking in any direction is OK. Seeding the space with a few of your own people pre-'seated' is helpful.

Think about the third dimension too – height. Use balloons, smoke, dry ice, glitter showers, streamers, exploding popping corn, a mirror ball, gauzes. Project onto the ceiling or high up on walls. Suspend, lower, raise, swing, drop things. When it comes to adding atmosphere, your imagination is the limit, not the space.

And don't overlook the outside of your building. Can people easily find their way in? How will you light the outside and the entrance? Will they be apprehensive about what they're coming into? Will you gather people in one place and have them come into the worship space together? Will people know what is expected of them when they arrive or enter? How? Are the toilets obvious? How will you make people feel welcome? I've visited many alternative worship services in New Zealand, Australia, the USA and the United Kingdom and very rarely have I been able to easily find the building, or the way into the building, or been shown where to go or what to do when I get inside. Recently I sat and waited for a service to start (it was late and without explanation) only to eventually discover I was on the wrong side of the projector screen! If it wasn't for the distance I'd travelled and my determination to find the service I would have given up and walked away on many occasions.

A little while ago, my answerphone had a message from a 25-year-old male. He said he wasn't a churchgoer or a Christian and he wanted to know if it would be all right if he came to church! 'Can anyone come? I'm not sure how church works. Let me know if I can just come along or not. Is this Sunday OK or do I need to wait until a proper time?' Those of us who have had even a brief encounter with the church easily forget how difficult the experience may be for someone fronting up for the first time. Great publicity is no substitute for a clear and helpful welcome.

The challenge is to integrate the space into your worship; to use it as part of the context you are curating, thereby reducing its tendency to be just a pictorial backdrop or at worst an undermining negative factor.

Projected Images and Screens

Pieces of fabric are wonderful for dividing up a large space, for providing colour and, best of all, for projecting onto. A slide or video projector can be projected onto almost any surface. The lighter the colour and smoother the surface the better. Walls, ceilings, people can all provide suitable surfaces. Bed sheets work fine. Worn bedsheets even work in place of expensive rear projection fabric allowing you either to have the projector out of the way behind the screen (assuming you haven't hung the screen on a wall!) or to view the projected image from both sides if the screen is hung centrally. Recently we tied four twelve-metre lengths of white sheet fabric (acquired from a sheet manufacturer) together at one end and hung it tent-like from the centre of the ceiling to the four walls. Punters sat around a central communion table inside this structure – while texts and images were projected onto the outside surfaces. The images were kept deliberately small and sharp.

It's well worth experimenting with cheap fabrics to see how they handle projected images. I recently discovered a translucent polyester sheet used by horticulturists to protect their crops from frost. It's 2 metres wide, comes in 100-metre rolls, works wonderfully as a rear projection material and costs one New Zealand dollar a metre. Projecting onto people can be fun too. I interviewed author Tom Sine about his view of the future while video images of traffic, housing, people, etc. were projected onto our light-coloured clothes and spilled onto the screen behind us. Mexican poncho style over-clothes of white fabric make great projection screens when the wearers hold their arms up. Lying on the floor while images are projected onto the ceiling can be relaxing in a more meditative style of service.

Use projectors to 'paint' your walls. Add features that couldn't be added any other way, e.g. a stained glass window high up on a wall. Project text of prayers or songs or slogans or scripture. Slide and video projectors are better than an overhead projector in most settings because they have less light spill and are more controllable. If you have to use an OHP, mask out all the unneeded areas of the transparency. Better still cut a negative of the image you want. Colour wash with coloured acetate or cellophane. Any colour other than white light is less harsh on the eyes.

Making Slides

You can easily make your own word slides to be projected too. Draw on clear acetate with an overhead transparency pen (permanent) or photocopy onto acetate (you may need to experiment to get the type reduced enough to fit into a 35mm slide frame). The ultimate in simplicity is to get a sheet of architect's tracing paper, cut it up into squares to fit your slide frame, then draw or write on it with pencils, or children's felt pens. If you have a camera, put some slide film in it and shoot your own images or photograph your computer screen with the words you want on it (PowerPoint is a useful source). Interesting effects can be produced by placing seeds and leaves between a layer of acetate and clear self-adhesive. Scratching the emulsion (duller) side of exposed film with a blunt nail or wire can produce quite adequate text slides, especially for one- or two-word slogans. You usually get a couple of frames suitable for this at the start and end of a roll of processed negatives. If you can't find any film to scratch, spray paint a sheet of clear acetate (use water-based spray). Colour with felt pens or cellophane.

Other more technical systems exist for making slides. I've just suggested some of the most basic. Combine two or three different techniques. Scrounge old slides from grandma's holiday collection. Advertise for them among your friends and work mates. Recycle old slide frames when possible and buy them from your local camera shop when it's not. Above all, give it a go. Produce your own still images for projecting. Borrow all the projectors you can find. Instead of turning the projector off when you don't want to use it during a service, put a black slide (use tinfoil or black film in a slide frame) in the carousel or cartridge.

When it comes to projecting images don't stick at just one projected onto one screen. Think about projecting text over a background slide, or even video (negative text, i.e. white text on black background is best for this). Visions alt.worship group in York have made an art form out of multiple projector images, using up to 12 slide projectors to create one huge image as a backdrop to their worship. You can see some of their work on their website at www.abbess.demon.co.uk/paradox/

Video

While you are logged on, www.trinity-bris.ac.uk/altwfaq/ has some excellent suggestions for using video in worship, and also reviews some resources. Video editing is now within the reach of most home computer owners and the results are limited only by your imagination and skill with the software. The development of DVD (Digital Video Disc) technology will open up the possibilities even further. There are the inevitable copyright considerations that need to be grappled with at the local level and appropriate decisions made there. No easy solution exists unless you live in the USA.[26]

The question of video projector versus multiple televisions is worth thinking about. I prefer multiple televisions as they seem warmer and more personal than a video projector image. They can also be spread around a space to create multiple foci or heaped in one place for an effect. A video projector creates more of a 'sit and watch' mentality and wherever the video screen is will inevitably become the de facto 'front' as far as punters are concerned. On the other hand, a video projector is much easier to set up than multiple televisions and gives a larger image. Multiple televisions can easily be connected using the RF (aerial) socket with cables, splitters, and small amplifiers (signal boosters) available at most electronics stores at very affordable prices. Despite the digital revolution there's plenty of years left yet in cathode ray tubes and RF connections. I recently saw a large jug of clear water placed in front of a television screen to create a very interesting effect as the image was viewed partially through the jug. Multiple video projectors can be used effectively with larger groups and don't always have to project large images. A small image in the corner of a screen or tucked away on a piece of wall can add to the atmosphere.

Image is Everything

Despite the phenomenal success of the Sprite drink campaign, 'Image is Nothing – Thirst is Everything', when it comes to communication in the emerging culture images are everything, and our thirst for them is insatiable. You could be forgiven for not realizing that if you spend most of your time in modern church buildings and services. A lecturer at the theological college I attended often said our theology today is 'off the wall', meaning we get it off the overhead projector screen, from our songs. What Western church building doesn't have an OHP screen? Many don't have much more than that to look at. Certainly not my Baptist church circles. This means that often worship is done in a sterile space that has minimal visual stimulation and communicates a message of 'outmoded', 'boring', 'unfulfilling'. It also means that many worshippers can't connect their life in an image-laden world with their Christian faith and worship.

I experienced this when doing some alt.worship with a large suburban congregation in New Zealand. The worship space was a bare, bland building with no Christian images or symbols anywhere. Not even a cross. Three hundred teenagers and young adults gathered to worship. As various images of a broken world moved over the screens and the Corrs track 'Forgiven, not Forgotten' rolled out of the speakers, a titter of giggling spread around the room. This group of 15- to 30-year-olds who lived with images and music every day of their lives – except Sunday – could not cope with making the same connections and interpretations in their worship. I met with 20 of them over the next few weeks to process the event. Worship and life were separate compartments for most. There were Christian images (which for them seemed to be limited to the cross and communion elements) and there were non-Christian images. There was no interaction or crossover between the two realms.

That approach doesn't work. It is time for the visual arts to come home where they belong – in the church. It's time to educate people about images and icons and symbols and use them to communicate the gospel to a visual culture. And I'm not talking about doves and rainbows cut out of felt stitched to a plain-coloured fabric wallhanging.

> Great care should be taken to avoid inserting 'bits of art' merely to decorate a blank wall, fill up an empty corner, or (worst of all) subject a worshipping community to doom and gloom by inserting yet more stained glass, that most overrated of all Christian art forms.[27]

I'm also not talking about worshipping images, but opening up the right side of the brain to join the rest of the body in worshipping God. For some people using any kind of images in worship is very difficult to cope with. After a very short and simple piece of worship at a Pentecostal Bible school, I had two men argue with me that using candles in worship was occultic. Thinking that this attitude may have come from their past involvement in such things I asked the question, which only proved to inflame the issue! Having no common ground for further discussion we agreed to differ and moved on. There is not much that can be done in those extreme situations.

The Spirit at Work

Parallel Universe ran a service based around thanking God for New Zealand (Kiwi) culture. Throughout the evening random slides of well-known paintings by NZ artists were projected onto three 6-metre wide screens that described the outer limits of the cavernous worship space. The paintings weren't religious in any way, just good Kiwi art. After the service two women came independently to the organizers and with tears in their eyes thanked us for using this art in the context of worship. They were artists or art students and recognized the paintings that they loved and appreciated. To have these paintings used in worship was such an affirmation that it was overwhelming for them. Their Christian faith had been connected to t-heir real worlds.

At a Quiet Service punters lay on the floor in the dark and reflected on slides of the crucifixion as painted by some of the Masters. Images remained for 4 or 5 minutes at a time over about an hour while the haunting Gavin Bryars' album *Jesus' Blood Never Failed Me Yet* was played. Many people experienced God's presence. One young woman wrote afterwards of the life-changing effect meeting with God in the combination of images and music had on her.

> I found last night's service extremely powerful and wanted to let you know how it touched me.
>
> First thing was that after about five minutes of lying there in the dark my inside person, which normally resides on a far-away planet, decided to be present. This is pretty unusual for me, and I enjoyed lying there feeling chock-a-block with myself, like after a big dinner.
>
> Then after about 25 times of the old man singing, it hit me like a ton of bricks that God actually loves me. I've always understood that God loves humanity and specific other people, but it's never really included me personally. I guess because I'm not usually present to receive any love … Anyway, what a revelation! Nice to have a good cry too.
>
> And then I had this picture of me on a beach. I've had this picture in the back (or front) of my mind since my dad left our family when I was a teenager. It's of him walking away from me and I'm a little kid running after him and screaming, and it's not making any difference.
>
> Anyway last night I was on the beach and it was the same old story – Dad walking away – but this time I was not running after him, but was turned the other way, facing God and His love.
>
> This is such a big deal to me. A definite step in the right direction. And I'd been feeling really discouraged yesterday about my screwiness and lack of progress mental health-wise.

God met with her. And I thought we were just showing a few images and playing some tracks!

'Stations of the Cross – Contemporary Icons to Meditate on at Easter' is an art installation that Cityside Baptist Church has put on the last three Easters. Up to 17 artists take an element of the final week of Jesus' life, e.g. Jesus is betrayed, Jesus before Pilate, Jesus is nailed to the cross, and interpret that in a visual medium of their choosing. Icons have been interactive, video-based, oil on canvas, calligraphy, sculpture, multimedia, found items, etc. The icons are arranged in a specially prepared space (described earlier) complete with original soundtrack in the background and notes to guide viewers. Very positive feedback has come from those inside the church and those outside it. One punter wrote how God had spoken to him, not through the great array and quality of the art but through the *Emergency Exit* sign indicating a door half way round the installation that was hidden by the art work. He said, 'I suddenly realised that Jesus could have exited his journey to the cross whenever he wanted to but he chose to continue on to the end.'

The Epicentre group in London run regular art exhibitions in pubs and public spaces as a means of engaging with the emerging culture and providing a Christian perspective on events and themes.[28]

Images and icons. Don't leave the church without them.

Symbols and Ritual Actions

A few years ago Parallel Universe worship took up the theme of God as fire. We explored five aspects:

1. The Fire of God's Presence (Exodus 3.2)
2. The Fire of God's Acceptance (Isaiah 6.7)
3. The Fire of Revealing (1 Corinthians 3.11)
4. The Fire of Suffering (1 Peter 1.7)
5. The Fire of Passion (Jeremiah 20.9)

The environment was set with large screens around the outer perimeter, a campfire circle of a dozen televisions in the centre surrounding a metre high gas flame (the TVs all showed video of fire). Punters sat around café tables with a candle on each. At the end of the night they took away red matchbooks with the five headings and scriptures printed on them. It was a wonderful service. As often happens some friends in another country took it and made it better. Here's how Cathy described Cafe Church's Night of Fire in an email.

It's time. The gathering of the tribes. I am really happy coz I see that some of our new attenders have brought their friends, and because I have spotted some old Cafe Churchers that I haven't seen in many moons. All the announcements happen up front. The end of the evening is reserved for prayer and stillness and gently yarning …

'At Cafe Church we use poems and metaphors and various kinds of images, and sounds and other things … to try to express our journey, and our searching through life and faith.

God does the same thing. Tonight is FIRE. God and his impact in our fragile world … in the events recorded in the Bible, and in the words of Jesus we find many symbols and images and metaphors … God trying to get through to us about what he thinks and who he is. Tonight we look at 5 different episodes involving fire. Connect at your level. Some of the passages may be familiar, but will be expressed in new ways, so that we too may find something new …'

On the tables are little folded papers with 5 of the passages printed.

Each table holds a candle, and a specially logoed matchbox for this night.

I will invite participation throughout. Get involved where you wish.

And so we begin.

'Prepare to worship …

Let us recognise the lives that we are in, the weeks that we have had, the moment all around us. Let us seek stillness, in each other's presence, and in the company of God himself …'

The slide on the wall reads 'Fire in the Dark'.

Tim begins a track from the CD *L'Apocalypse des Animaux* (Vangelis. Wonderful). After a time I pray out loud, asking God to meet here with us.

Tim fires up the data projector and a massive fire begins licking across the wall.

New slide 'Fire of God's Presence'. I read the words … 'Take off your shoes … We stand before the fire of God's presence …'[29] At the conclusion of this first piece, I invite the people to take a match, ignite it from the candle on the centre of their table, and say together 'The fire of God here with us'.

These phrases and the titles are slides: white text on black, projected just over the video fire.

For part 2 'The Fire of God's Acceptance' I invite everyone outside. As I read of Isaiah's coal kissing encounter, Tim carries a burning coal around the group. I hand out 3 candles, and ask the people to pass them on, saying the words 'The fire of God's acceptance'…

It isn't raining very much!

Back inside for James and 'The Fire of Revealing'. James is really mad and very theatrical. He is passionate and wild. He rips into these words. While he does, Tim flashes up a great series of images – advertisements, TV stuff, news shots of destruction, conmen, people … At the end, when James is explaining that all the rubbish gets burnt up, he flames the paper from which he has been reading, and waves it around.

The Fire of Suffering. Peter Gabriel's *Zaar* moans from the speakers.

Slide of words appear on the wall. I ask everyone to read them and contemplate them. 'It is difficult to live, and to escape pain. If we follow Jesus …' Well … I invite everyone to say these words together: 'Lord God, you are above and beyond all things, your nature is to love … We hurt …' As I read the list of our afflictions: cancer, AIDS, car crash, depression, sexual abuse, schizophrenia…I think about these people around me. Yes indeed. I am glad to be acknowledging the sufferings that I know they have had…we have.

I complete the reading:

'…and the answer was a

long

time

coming.'

Last stage: The Fire of Passion.

The image of the fire continues to blaze before us.

I read the opening stanzas. The people read together the conclusion 'The word of the Lord is a fire in my heart, and a hammer in my bones … Fire of God we welcome you.'

We ignite our last matches.

I pause. I'm searching for something. What's needed now?

I say: 'If I began to sing a song unaccompanied, would people know it?

"In our darkness, there is no darkness … In you oh Lord, the deepest night is clear as the day light. In our darkness …"' Beautiful lilting of sounds arising from the people, over and over, and around and around …

'May you take away something sacred and holy and new … go with God …'

And so, the Lord is revealed. In our presence he is present.

Hilary told me that she really liked singing at the end. And that she really valued the acknowledgement of the pain and cynicism and all the bad stuff. Lu said that she got into many conversations about the Holy Spirit as fire, and his presence at Cafe Church, and how we could go forward, and how others are feeling about this …

Ruth says that the night is a masterpiece, and that she has had heaps of good conversations. Rick says that: 'Sometimes, you know, sometimes, God is so big.' I do love Rick.

Connections

In Montreal late in the evening of Gay and Lesbian Pride Day a young man started arranging hundreds of candles in the street. The glow attracted a crowd and without need for any announcement, a large group gathered and started 'praying'. Some sat, some stood and held each other, some knelt down and lit candles with him. People laid badges, flowers, cards, whatever. No-one needed to be told the candles were for people with AIDS – everyone knew. The young man had created sacred space, had brought us all into silent attendance and into solidarity. He had created time for safe sharing of tears, and had involved people in a transforming ceremony.

A very different setting but a no less powerful use of symbols and ritual occurred at a Visions service in London. I sat through the very well curated service, reasonably uninvolved. I was distracted from entering fully into the worship by my bad habit of noticing how things were being done and how the service was shaped and progressing. Until we came to the Prayer Ritual. We were invited to come forward and pick up a brick as a symbol of a burden we wanted to bring to God. We processed around the space carrying our brick, talking with God. As the circuit brought us back to the front of the space the brick was exchanged for a glass of water symbolising meeting Jesus who shares our burdens. As I walked forward to pick up my brick I burst into tears. From distant observer to involved participant in a few steps. I was very aware of God's presence in those few minutes.

When Third Sunday Service wanted worshippers to evaluate where they were on their journey with Christ they asked them to place a thumb-printed sticker on the outside of an igloo tent with candles burning inside it. The distance from the lit centre indicating your felt relationship distance.

Symbols can take many forms and may be material objects or symbolic gestures. If your group meets regularly you may find it helpful to establish some regular rituals and symbols. These build community, help to remind you of your communal journey and enable deeper involvement in the meaning of the symbol as less effort is concentrated on figuring out what to do. The danger is always that there may come a time when the ritual has only form and no meaning.

> There was once a teacher of great faith and insight. Several disciples gathered around him to learn from his wisdom. It so happened that each time the small community met for prayer, the cat would come in and distract them. The teacher ordered the cat tied whenever the community prayed. Eventually the great one died, but the cat continued to be tied up at worship time. When the cat died, another cat was bought to make sure that the teacher's wishes were still faithfully observed. Centuries passed, and learned treatises were written by scholarly disciples on the liturgical significance of tying up a cat while worship is performed.[30]

One of the most helpful aspects of ritual actions and the use of stations, icons or symbols as part of worship is that they can be used to encourage movement and interaction on the part of worshippers. Punters are no longer passive listeners but become active participants. Movement also reminds us that we are a journeying people, a pilgrim people.

Silence

This may be the best place to make a comment about silence. Richard Giles said, 'If nature abhors a vacuum, the English at worship abhor space, with silence coming a close second.' His reference to space was alluding to the desire to clutter worship spaces with furniture and objects. Silence is often crowded out too. Contemporary culture is not good at providing silence. Perhaps it is afraid of what it might hear or that it will hear nothing if it stops long enough to listen. In Christian worship we need to stop in order to let God speak and to listen to what God has to say, as well as to our own selves. We need time to hear what has been said in the liturgy and in Scripture. To digest and 'hear' it. Silence should be used in an incidental way to provide space and pace between elements of the service, i.e. by not rushing from one element to the next, and also in a more deliberate and measured way to provide significant periods of shared silence. Many people will not be used to this and parameters may need to be set. Tell them how long the silence will be (start with a few minutes) and make the start and end very clear. People also need to know what they should be doing during the silence. Are they reflecting on a piece of scripture, talking to God, Listening to God, or thinking about something in particular.

Heavenly Bodies

The most readily available and accessible worship tool is your body. High tech and low cost (to use in worship anyway). Find ways of having the body work for you and not against you, i.e. numb on a pew. Postures and ritual actions are the most obvious uses, and many suggestions for these have already been made. Kneeling, sitting, lying, standing, hands clasped, head bowed, walking, hands outstretched, shifting gaze are all active ways to see the body as more than a passive container for the mind and eyes. The simple act of having a reader speak from the 'back' of the space or a slide projected to the 'side' causes bodies to move.

Bodies need to be given encouragement to move, as well as space and opportunity. Music helps this. A change in aural landscape, e.g. from silence to music, from soft to loud, from reflective to up tempo accompanied by verbal instructions such as an invitation to move to a prayer wall and write up prayers or take bread and wine, makes the moving much easier. People hesitate to move during silence unless they know each other very well, the instructions are very unambiguous, and the task not too threatening. Changes in the background noise provide a subtle signal for people to move.

Dancing is an obvious use of the body in worship. Not 'worship dance' but full-blooded saturation in whatever music style you like to move to. Dancing as an act of celebration and abandonment. If your punters aren't quite up to that, get them to stand and stamp their feet or sway in time to a track you play. Walking while singing also works well, especially if the lyrics are projected onto screens around the space. Don't let everyone move in the same direction. Move randomly. Walking toward and past and behind someone who is singing is a wonderful experience. Especially if parts are being sung unaccompanied. Where I worship we use Taize and Iona Chants, but mostly original one-liners with three or four different lines sung simultaneously.[31]

Have punters write on their hands, make palm prints on a banner or wall, anoint each other on the forehead or back of a hand (depending on the level of familiarity) with the sign of the cross, wash and dry each other's or your own hands or feet in warm scented water. Incense is the most obvious source of olfactory stimulation. Use proper church incense rather than the very sweet-smelling joss sticks type. Walk around with it in a thurible of some sort (a baked bean can on chains works well) or in a bowl so that you can cense the worshippers directly rather than just have a general wafting of this symbolic presence of the Spirit. Recently a punter described his experience of being censed as the part of the service when God spoke most clearly to him about being near regardless of his feelings. After taping torn out newspaper headlines on the walls as our cries to God for our world, we had someone walk around waving incense onto the cuttings as she read out the headlines and acknowledged that God had heard our prayers. 'God knows the "6000 dead in Turkish Earthquake"; the cries of "Farmers Suffering in Drought" are heard by God …'

Bodies should always be affirmed in and by our worship. This can be more difficult to achieve than it seems and what is affirming for one person can be threatening and upsetting for another. Even a simple action like handwashing (let alone footwashing) can be boundary-invading for some people, particularly if the group does not have much relationship or history. Also, the context can dramatically alter the appropriateness and meaning-value of an action. For example a shoulder-rub among a dozen adults around a campfire at the end of a weekend retreat will feel a lot different to one among a congregation of 250 in a Methodist Church on a Sunday morning. The same principles of context and community that apply to music and images and symbols also apply to how you use the body in worship.

Whatever you do in worship, find ways to involve the body and as many of its senses as possible.

Creativity

Welcome to the magical, shadowy underworld of creativity … well it often seems like that to those who think they don't have a creative cell in their body. If you believe that's you, you've been deceived. Don't believe it.

Creativity is not the same as artistic ability. You can be creative without being able to paint, draw, sculpt, dance or play an instrument. Creativity is also not something that you either have or you don't; a gene you're either given at birth or you miss out on. Any person can be more creative than they are (or become creative if they're not). You can develop a creative outlook.

Creativity is not about creating. That is a task we leave to God alone. God has an advantage over us. God spoke and it came into being. We re-create, or recombine elements that have already been created. So half the task is already done for us! You're already half-way there the moment you begin. God's creativity is the basis for our creativity. We put already created elements together in new ways to 'create' something new. So for us, creativity is primarily about seeing new relationships between elements – such as when we use stones to symbolize the hard parts of our lives that need to be softened by God. For us there is nothing totally new, only new combinations of old elements.

Begin to think about your creativity as finding new ways of combining existing things. New ways of putting old ideas or practices together. Get away from thinking of creativity as having to come up with totally new things – *de nouveau* (out of nothing). Creativity never comes out of nothing. It always comes out of what you have previously seen, heard or experienced. If you think you're uncreative, you're not, you've just never worked hard enough at developing creative new connections between things.

Creativity is all around you and part of the essence of who you are. God's Spirit, the creator Spirit, the Spirit of Creativity lives and works within you. God's resources are available to you. Your creativity starts in you. It isn't something external. It reflects who you are and is fed and informed by your experiences and how you process them. Creativity is something you are before it's something you do, and you can be more creative.

A STARTING POINT

A good place for starting is to look at the programme, talk, service, sermon, whatever it is you are preparing and ask yourself, 'What would I like to see happen here? What's possible?'

Maybe that was what the Godhead asked when they looked on a messed-up creation and humankind and decided to re-create out of worse-than-nothing. When you ask that question you begin to get to the core of what you're trying to achieve. With that knowledge you can decide what is helpful or unhelpful in moving towards your goal in a particular situation.

A golden rule is to imagine in bright flashy neon in front of your mind's eye constantly ... I have not taught something if no one has learnt anything.

What ever you do – no matter how poorly and inadequately – will always communicate something. It will probably be the opposite of what you intended, but it will communicate. If you have a clear understanding of what you want to achieve – The 'What would I like to see happen here?' question – then you can not only sort out what is helpful from what is not, but you'll also be able to evaluate the success or not of your creativity in this instance. The brightest, flashiest, most creative event in the world is wasted if it doesn't communicate what you set out to communicate. (I know there are arguments against what I've just said, but you get the point.) I hope to encourage you not only to be more creative, but to be able to hone and focus your creativity so that it hits the spot you want it to – like a laser in surgery, just the right amount of creativity, in the right direction at the right moment.

> Each person is creative in different ways, but everyone can be creative in some way; the gifts of the spirit are for all Christians.[32]

> Our obedience and surrender to God are in large part our obedience and surrender to our gifts. This is the message ... of the parable of the talents. Our gifts are on loan. We are responsible for spending them in the world.[33]

DEVELOPING A CREATIVE OUTLOOK

Look for another way to skin the cat. Think about new possibilities and new uses for familiar objects. Creativity is always an experience. It is knowledge and information dressed up as experience. Creativity makes knowledge more accessible, it helps people experience truth. So having decided what you want to communicate (the outcome, not the content) ask your self how you can best have your audience take that away with them. What are the ways this could happen? How can you best arrange the content and responses to bring that about?

EXPOSE YOURSELF

Observe other people's creativity. Participate in it. Throw yourself into life. Don't always listen to the music, go to the films, read the magazines that you're familiar and comfortable with. Go outside your comfort zone. Visit art galleries, particularly installation art. Make new friends. Go to new places at different times. Keep pushing the boundaries of your experience. Reflect on these new experiences. Analyse what you see/hear/experience. Ask yourself why and how others achieved the effect they did.

PUSH THE EDGES

You need to be willing to take a few risks to be creative. Using the track 'Firestarter' by the Prodigy to communicate an aspect of the work of the Holy Spirit may offend some people. It may also communicate to some others. Only you will know your audience and their boundaries. You also have to know your own. Both need gentle pushing at times if any worthwhile change is to come in people's lives. You also need to check out your motives from time to time.

WORK AT IT

Creativity is developed by practice and hard work. The more you work at it (if you reflect on what you have done) the better you become. No one ever learnt to ride a bike by reading a book about it. Likewise to be creative you must get out and do it. Reading the books can inform your journey, but you need to be on the journey first.

I heard an interview with musicians the Chemical Brothers. One said, 'We've been very lucky', and the other one responded very quickly 'No we haven't! The more you practice, the luckier you get.' He was right. Much of the work of creativity is wading through stuff you toss out on the way to the idea that you finally use.

Work with others wherever possible. There is much more creativity in two or three people bouncing ideas around than there is in you thinking alone. Other people also help you to see if an idea is workable and appropriate, and may give you the confidence to move ahead with an idea when you wouldn't have if you were on your own.

MAKE MISTAKES

The best teacher is your mistakes. (Although if you find yourself making nothing else you should seek advice!) No one likes making mistakes in public – and all creativity has at least an element of public exposure to it. It is this fear of public failure that kills creativity.

Fear of criticism – the real killer. Nothing saps creativity like criticism. Hear it; evaluate it; learn from it; walk away from it.

Fear of failing – failure is never final. It can be helpful in stemming overconfidence and complacency and uncreative reuse.

Fear of sinning – what better reason to risk this than in some creative endeavour! There's always grace.

Fear of the unknown – confront it head on.

Fear of embarrassment – ask yourself why? What is the worst thing that could happen to you?

Fear of being misunderstood – plan to not have it happen.

All of these are reasonable fears and need to be acknowledged as such. You could fall into any one or more of these holes, but you take a step forward in your creativity when you recognize the dangers, and don't let them paralyse you. These dangers can be minimized by preparing carefully, making sure you understand the setting you will be operating in, by giving clear and adequate explanation of what is expected of your audience, and sometimes by giving advance warning of what is coming up. (Nothing can guarantee that after all that you won't still be criticized.)

EVALUATE

Reflect on what you do. Ask for feedback from unlikely people. Evaluate the outcomes in relation to what you wanted to achieve. Avoid self-justification. Learn from your critics. Keep notes on what worked and what didn't and why. File your running orders, scripts and notes so you can come back and read them later. This can remind you of what you've done previously and also spark new ideas and possibilities. And remember 'If at first you do succeed – try not to be totally overwhelmed by your success!'

TRUST YOUR INSTINCTS BUT HAVE HUMILITY

It is difficult to trust one's own creativity, to remain open to images and symbols emerging out of one's journey with the Spirit. Many of us have learned to discount our own perceptions, our own truths, especially if we have grown up in families where we were abused and silenced or in schools where every peg was supposed to fit in the same sized hole. We may have internalised social values that deny women's right to shape the language of prayer; or, we may have believed the myth that real men don't develop their creativity. Perhaps, too, we have accepted values that keep us too busy to cultivate a relationship with God or to listen truths for emerging with us. Finding our own creative voice, surfacing our own images, experiences, and perceptions, can be difficult, yet rewarding.[34]

Trust your instincts as to what will work, but never (or at least rarely!) set out to deliberately offend people. Constantly keep in mind what your ultimate aim is. This will often mean that you have to sacrifice your best, most creative idea – because it simply doesn't advance your current purpose.

PLAY

Play – with ideas and objects. Make new connections. Try 'what ifs'. Become like a child and discover new connections between familiar things. If nothing is working, go away and come back to it later. Ask yourself, 'What wouldn't work in this situation?' 'What wouldn't I do?'

FEEL THE PAIN

Creativity comes out of who you are. It isn't just 'what you do'. Allowing yourself to experience the emotional lows of life as well as the highs is an important part of developing your creativity. It builds depth, substance and empathy. Don't be surprised when an idea that seemed superb two weeks ago suddenly seems to be weak and inconsequential the day before it's due to be delivered. Trust your original instincts and allow yourself to doubt, and feel uncertain about its validity. Going ahead, or deciding on good reasons why you shouldn't, are part of gaining experience in creativity. There is no substitute for these experiences. You must go through them and not look for a way around them. Avoiding pain in creativity inevitably leads to mediocrity.

VITAL INGREDIENTS

Two vital ingredients for developing creativity are space and process. Creativity takes time to develop. It can't be rushed. It must be given room to brew. Often this time also requires a place. It's difficult to be creative when under pressure of time or space or people.

Process is also important. Any creative event you participate in is the end result of a process. A process that relates to a specific time and place and purpose. You are participating as a consumer of the end result of that process. Resist the temptation to be only a consumer. It's great for ideas and stimulation but your own process is vital if you're to shape an element or event that will communicate your purpose, in your setting, to your audience. It's often in this process that you have to choose between options, fine-tuning them with your overall purpose in mind. Minimalism is usually better than overkill. Again, the process may mean that you leave your best idea out because the shape of the event has moved away from that direction. Tough calls to make but a vital part of the process of creativity.

Conclusion

When worship preparation is seen as an art, as an experience to be wisely and lovingly curated; when its shape, style and content develops from the context of the lives of the community coming to worship; when thought is given to incorporating the total environment and all the senses in the worship experience, then worship that encourages a loving of God with heart, soul, mind and strength will be hard to avoid. Go for it. Your experiences will be important in funding new possibilities for the shape of the future church.

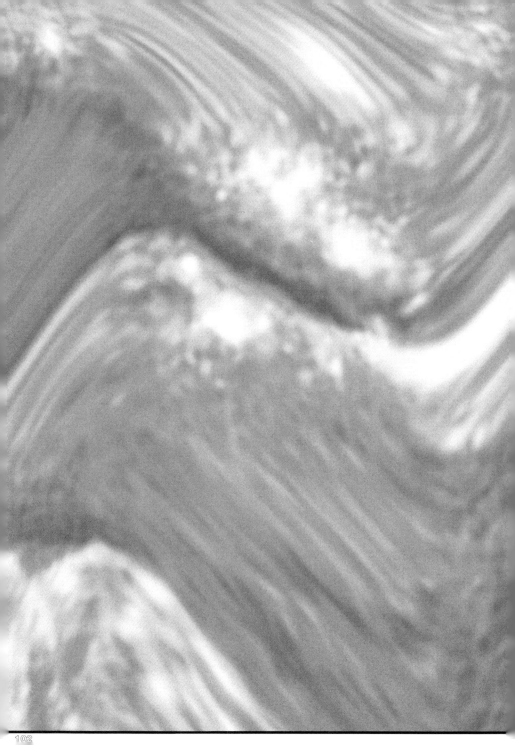

In this chapter we listen to a selection of stories from groups which have ventured into the unknown. On the CD-ROM, you'll find even more accounts of new ventures from The Epicentre Network, the Spine Community, Plunge, Spirited Exchanges, Third Sunday Service, Graceway, Nine O'clock Community, Spirited Con-versations, and Pathways Church. These stories have been written by the people involved. They are their stories and reflect the diversity of style, approach and outcome that are possible when creativity and Christ-ian faith are mixed with frustration and desperation. Not content to just knock the Church or opt out they have struggled to give birth to alternatives. We are grateful to the writ-ers and their groups for exposing themselves to the world in this way. Most groups can be contacted through the address attached or websites listed in the Resources: Services, Churches and Groups section.

" I think that we are standing on a watershed. Times of transition. Times of earthquake and tidal wave. Things that go bump in the night, and skies that explode overhead. I think that the big church is in for an even bigger shock.

ckp
"

Grace (London, UK)

Step into the Gothic cavern of St Mary's Anglican Church in Ealing, west London, and walk down the candle-lit aisle towards the screen which fills the sanctuary arch. Sit on the floor in the soft light of the projected words and images. Videos loop silently on TVs, candles shine all around. It is beautiful, numinous.

Laid-back dance music shapes the atmosphere like a movie soundtrack. The purpose of the strange installations is not immediately apparent. You will soon be making something, contemplating something, smelling or eating something, writing or reading, feeling objects, processing around, planting things, burning paper or incense – who knows? This is not a worship show and you are not just a passive audience. Welcome to Grace.

The Grace story begins in the early 90s, when Mike Rose, desperately bored with standard evangelical worship, had taken to leading the youth group just to escape from church services. Both he and the curate Mike Starkey had been to Nine O'Clock Service and were interested in the possibilities of 'alternative worship'; and because curates don't stay long in one church there was an incentive to take action rather than waiting on church committees. They gathered a small group of people with creative gifts, planned a twice-monthly series of services and hoped that someone would come. There was no budget but they had decided anyway that the best approach was to keep it small and manageable and produce services that they could take their friends to. Rose had been concerned at the huge drop in church attendance by young people, but

> perhaps more than that it was a self-centered act. I knew that if things didn't change for me there was a good chance that the reality chasm between my life and my church would become so big that one side would win (and I didn't reckon it would be church).

The first service was in November 1993. The team had asked everyone they could think of, an unknown pastor called Dave Tomlinson was due to speak about the subject 'Grace', and the service started when everyone had arrived. It contained many elements still used by Grace today – 'homemade' music, visuals and liturgy; plenty of ambient and chilled out music to accompany readings and prayers; and a sense of freedom and space to explore God in different ways. Mike Rose:

> It was brilliant. The room was crap, poor lights, terrible sound and total lack of musical genius but I knew something had been born. Church was no longer something that happened to me but something I could take responsibility for. There didn't need to be a conflict between the rest of the week and Sunday. I was proud of my church for the first time since I was a child watching my Dad preach!!!

The second service had a comedian as its star turn and the team arranged the church hall as a comedy club (and tried to write worship songs about humour). They created a 'love grotto' when feminist theologian Elaine Storkey spoke, and have several times turned the church into a sort of café in order to feed more than the mind. Throughout, Grace has had a sense of humour and has been about taking reverent risks.

In the summer of 1995 Mike Starkey left for a new post and Mike Rose was suffering from total burnout. Of the five original team members, three had left St Mary's and another wanted to step down. They'd run out of energy and ideas and Grace had a holiday. In the meantime Jonny and Jenny Baker had arrived at St Mary's to work for Youth for Christ in London, bringing fresh ideas, songwriting talents and contacts which would resource Grace and enable it to become a resource for other churches. A new team emerged and Grace returned in January 1996 in a monthly format which was easier to manage.

In the years since then it has made several appearances on TV and provided worship at Greenbelt and other festivals. In May 1999 we took part in the Archbishop of Canterbury's millennium youth weekend 'The Time of Our Lives', culminating in a service for 500 in Southwark Cathedral visited by the Archbishop himself. Services have been about art, rage, prejudice, liberation, the future, ecology, wonder, holiness and anything else that engages our concern. In autumn 1998 we began holding Eucharist services each month in addition to our 'normal' services; these are on a reduced scale to avoid overloading the team. They have enabled us to explore the meaning and practice of the sacrament and have become a successful and important aspect of Grace.

Grace has its ups and downs. It's not always easy to be original, or to find the time, or the energy. It can be disheartening when we go to huge effort and few people turn up; but we find that for us and for those who do turn up the sense of God's presence makes it all worthwhile. It has become an exciting and relevant part of our lives, as worship should be. We hope that God has been glorified and that Grace does, and will, play a part in building his kingdom.

Mike Rose/Steve Collins
freespace.virgin.net/adam.baxter/grace
Email: grace.london@btinternet.com

Cityside Baptist Church and the Parallel Universe (Auckland, New Zealand)

A newspaper reporter filed this report:

Cityside Baptist Church, in Mt Eden, Auckland is not your average New Zealand Baptist Church, simply because the majority of its community of 120 adults are under 35 years of age. The church has no teenagers, and only a handful of young children.

The church's history goes back to the 1880s, when it was known as Mount Eden Baptist. It later became the City Mission church, with its membership peaking at about 150 members (250 in Sunday school) during World War I. But numbers started declining after 1945, and at one stage (1960) the church shut down altogether.

Today Cityside Baptist Church, as the City Mission Church has been called for the last few years, has become well known in Auckland for the creativity of its worship services, and its attempts to interact with the culture of the inner city.

It's a church with a difference.

Pastor Mark Pierson makes a point of giving members the room for risk, failure and participation. Effort is emphasised rather than achievement, and questions are encouraged.

The Parallel Universe is an innovative ministry of the church that began six years ago to experiment with a different style of worship.

The comments about Cityside are fairly accurate but Parallel Universe was never seen as an 'experiment'. It was an attempt to provide a worshipping community for 25-to-45-year-olds who either had dropped out of the mainstream church or had never seen the gospel as relevant to their lives. Services were held in various bars and nightclubs around the area and involved using a lot of projected images – slide and video – and both live and recorded music. We were doing worship as we liked it – with the images and music we related to.

At the same time Cityside was defining what it was about and shaping how it would do things. No master plan or five-year goals. Just a desire to be a community of faith where you could be yourself, ask your questions, talk about your successes and failures, and where the worship services resourced people for living as Christians day to day. Real and without pretence or presumption. Asking 'why' before we asked 'how'.

As the Cityside church has evolved it has incorporated and drawn into its life the principles and people that were Parallel Universe. So an average month sees a weekly morning service that involves a large amount of participation both from the various rostered leaders of the service and the congregation. Singing doesn't have a high profile and it isn't unusual for us not to sing at all, or to sing songs and chants unaccompanied. Evening services currently run on a monthly cycle – Labyrinth Worship, Story Telling night, and Quiet Service (which may be replaced by a Not So Quiet Service).

We're very committed to engaging with contemporary culture, particularly through the arts, and to trying to figure out some meaningful ways of doing church with those who've not found the mainstream church scene helpful. Our engagement with the culture involves us in an annual Easter Art Installation – Stations of the Cross: Contemporary Icons to Reflect on at Easter – some involvement with a café in the red light district, and with our local prison. There is little formal structure at Cityside and decisions are generally made by consensus. We have no money beyond paying for the very basics so decision-making is simplified! We employ only a pastor.

Citysiders have 24-hour access to our building and we have established a workroom with various multimedia gear, slide copying, video editing, etc. available to anyone who wants to use it for art or doing CVs and job applications.

We struggle financially as well as to know how we should best involve the young children of our congregation in our life. Our buildings are too small and no longer suit us but moving takes resources that we don't seem to have. We have more ideas than we have energy. So there are issues to keep working with as we press forward. Cityside is primarily Citysiders – the people. They are such great people to be around and to share life with at the start of a new millennium, that the problems seem insignificant.

Mark Pierson
Email: info@cityside.org.nz

Vaux (London, UK)

Ice, water and steam are all different 'phases' of the same material. Ice is hard and easy to grasp, but cold. Water is easy to stomach. Steam is difficult to handle – the most highly energised: perhaps the most useful yet most dangerous phase. At the point where the material takes on a new structure, a phase change occurs.

It seems to us at Vaux that the West in general, and the church as a part of that, is in the midst of a phase change. New modes of communication and understanding truth are appearing and, more importantly, old ones are disappearing. Not everyone will discern this change of phase – some see only water, while others feel the heat and need something more freeing.

Vaux is perhaps a bridging post for those experiencing that change. It finally came to expression in November '98 after an extended period of dissatisfaction with the modes of worship the church was using. We felt that the old phase – the rituals, codes and expressions – were now strange to us. It was becoming 'increasingly bizarre and abstract' and everything had 'long since ceased to resonate.' Not that God was losing his meaning, more that the church was failing to represent accurately the realities of that relationship as we experienced it. It seemed that the real questions were not being answered and that truth was not being sought. Radical speech had turned to crafted oratory, and heartfelt, sacrificial worship to slick, band-led pop. And all this while people struggled and suffered in silence … we heard 'peace, peace, but there was no peace'.

In 587 BC God dismantled the known world in Israel. The temple was destroyed, the people displaced into exile and all public life ended. This was a massive 'phase change' for them: everything their faith had relied on was destroyed. God's actions were not immediately obvious – some of the prophets did not discern what God was doing, but others did and helped the community, through their poetry, to make two crucial and difficult moves: to relinquish the old order, and to receive the new. At the end of the twentieth-century it may be that God is dismantling our known world of Enlightenment thinking, of economic madness, and doing something new. I guess through our art we at Vaux are trying to work at that difficult interface of relinquishing the old and receiving the new.

Part of the relinquishing process has to be to grieve for the old order. We found that much of our early output was quite dark and painful. This has been cathartic and essential. To deny the pain of the past would be to allow it to fester until some future time. One of our number is a trained art therapist and has helped greatly in facilitating expression of hurt and hope. Only now perhaps are we beginning to see more 'up' stuff coming through.

As a group we are very much in our infancy and little has been defined. However, we do sense that creativity is our main tool and it is by being creative that we will aid the reception of the new. This has taken many forms, deliberately drawing on the gifts that people involved have. We have integrated video, music, slides, dance, silence, poetry, painting, ice sculpture, liturgy, songs, meditation, information, intercession, food, beers, etc. – all pretty standard alternative worship fodder! One way that we might describe ourselves is as being 'worship architects' – designing spaces within which people can worship. They are planned and thought out, they draw on all sorts of traditions, yet hopefully don't dictate exactly how people must worship within them. So we encourage contributions of any format or media to enhance the space.

It has not always been an easy journey. Part of the sacrifice of doing what we do is that we have stepped out of a very lively church full of 'our sort of people' into a tiny congregation of people we may not naturally get along with. However, we saw it as essential to do that: the Vicar of this church had offered us the space to use – a huge Victorian high Anglo-Catholic place – and we felt it would be wrong to simply rock up there once a month to do our stuff without committing to the rest of the people who worshipped there. So we go (almost!) every Sunday morning and join them for sung Eucharist; one of us is now on the PCC and we are on the coffee rota, etc. – in some ways a huge step back for us in order that we can move on. And the congregation has continued to amaze us with their generosity and support. They have never questioned or judged and many have come to our services and contributed. The integrity of the Vicar's support was recently shown on St Peter's Day – one of the most important Sundays for them – when we were asked to do the 'sermon slot' in the morning service and told strictly that we weren't to tone anything down for them!

We also continue to struggle with how to keep what we do as open as possible, with as many people as possible contributing, yet without losing the purity of the vision; we learned the hard way in one very hectic service we did for Jubilee 2000! We think we will now appoint a 'director' for each service who will make final decisions about what is working and what isn't to keep the focus. We normally meet together a couple of weeks before the service, eat some food, pray, drink some beers and bat ideas around. We might then agree that someone is going to make a video, someone else write something, and someone else lead a meditation … we perhaps meet up again the week before and put it in some kind of order, then just meet a couple of hours beforehand to set up. We normally don't know the details of what others have prepared, so we basically bring what we have done as a gift to one another to aid our worship. That emphasis on generosity has been key, and is a powerful deterrent to stressing about perfection, smoothness and cost.

Vaux has become for us, then, a place where maybe we can begin to represent truthfully our relationships with God. Where we can create a meaningful dialogue between God, ourselves and our culture. It is a place where we can, without guilt or reproach, honestly express the tension we feel we live under as we attempt to relinquish one world order and receive a new one. But we also want Vaux to have a prophetic edge, to aid the relinquishing of the capitalist, materialist, McDonaldalized culture and proactively try to receive and nurture the new order of justice and a transformed society. It is far more than a service, and exists primarily in the relationships that have grown massively as we have worked together on worship. We feel we have hardly started, and that is exciting … it's also important, because people need to know that it is not beyond their reach to do something similar.

Email: TheVaux@aol.com

The Meeting Tent (Derby, UK)

It's hard to see now exactly where we went wrong. From the start we had an emphasis on creating a quality worship experience within a club setting and within club culture. We were able to use an actual nightclub, and used tunes from contemporary club culture. We thought we had something really good going on but this is not a success story –

Derby, England is a fairly modern town that qualifies as a city by virtue of having both a cathedral and a university – neither of which is over 50 years old. In many ways it is a fairly traditional place – but there is a significant youth population and a thriving night life. On Friday and Saturday nights the town centre heaves with young people – cruising, drinking, clubbing. Derby has had one of the United Kingdom's most notable venues (Progress) for over five years. Just the place then for an alternative worship venue.

What about the church? Well the churches in the city get together in a number of ways and are prepared to support ecumenical activities. Both the Anglican bishop, and the university chaplain were supportive of the idea, and a group of church leaders was approached to act as a 'council of reference'. The main leaders of the idea were a curate with experience gained at a nearby, but now significantly different project 'Be Real', youth workers from a large Anglican church, Youth With A Mission, and a Pentecostal church, and an ex-attender of the Warehouse, in York. All of us were prepared to work with an open-ended agenda – and not to attempt this as an 'evangelistic outreach'. We wanted to offer a service to the church and the wider community.

We met and worked and prepared a quality product, combining visuals, slides, liturgy, and of course music. The intention was to create a service that would fit into the club culture, using existent music (some re-editing) of a vaguely house/ trance/ambient style. Definitely a dance vibe, but an opportunity to worship within that format. We used a professional artist to create the logo and other graphics for the service. It was good. We found and worked on tunes – many of which we could lift directly from dance CDs. We worked on the ambience of the place – creating screens to give a 'tent' feel (The meeting tent name comes from the tabernacle where Moses met God and experienced God's glory). We obtained slide projectors and incense burners and turned the nightclub into something special.

So what happened? All along we had been aware of the need for 'critical mass' – the necessary number of participants to make the event take off. We had appointed one of the leaders as publicity person, and they had worked at linking with youth groups, university Christian groups, and churches, as well as producing fliers for distribution through record shops, boutiques, etc. We had at every stage tried to involve young people in the decision-making and creative processes – aware that those of us in our late 20s and 30s did not have the same awareness of club culture. Our success in all this was limited.

We met a large degree of incomprehension and apathy. There were some who were interested, but many who were happy with the diet of folk songs they were fed in their churches, and who could not see the possibility before them. Even those Christians who did go clubbing generally went to places playing chart music.

Similarly, we were not able to get our non-Christian clubbing contacts to believe that we might have something worth committing themselves to. In the end we ran on four occasions – achieved our creative goals, but never brought in enough punters/worshippers. The nightclub manager was letting us use the club for free by the end – he thought it was a worthwhile event. But our turnout was too low (tens and twenties) to make it worthwhile.

Our other reflection was that we still expected people to come to us – although we were in a nightclub and not a church, it was still our ground and not others'. The basic mission principle is to go to where others are and value what they have. If we had been able to continue we would have found ways to get into the clubs and build a community within them – then see what grew out of that. As it was we just didn't have the necessary time to devote to such a demanding work and our team folded.

Neil Elliot
Email: rev.nelli@virgin.net

Glenbrook Community Church

We started with a vision to run a family church. A place where kids and adults could worship together. A church without all the energy-sapping programmes and meetings that inevitably dull the flame behind the eyes of otherwise radical followers. We wanted to be a community of believers where tired and sick people could come for rest and healing. A place where our spirituality is as normal and central in our community life as sexuality is in marriage. We wanted to be a Christian group that is transparent and honest making a difference in the community at large. We have been a community for seven years now and I am often asked how it is going. Sometimes I reflect on the life of our church family and am overjoyed, our vision has materialized, lives are changing, grand opportunities beckon, new gifts are emerging and everyone just seems to sing in tune. At other times I anguish and fret and worry wondering if God even knows we exist.

Glenbrook is a semi-rural community south of Auckland, of 1,600 people largely made up of young families living on 'lifestyle blocks' (small acreages and hobby farming). The majority of adults have a pioneering type spirit searching for a good place to raise a family. Most were totally immunized against church by regular injections of starchy religion during their childhood. We gathered a home group of locals together over a two-year period. When it came time to go public we hired a small sports bar at the park where services were held for the next four years. We eventually outgrew the clubrooms and now meet in the community hall.

The church meets three Sundays out of four. On the fourth week we have a Friday night service. Our Sunday services are compilations of offerings from a rostered congregation. Last Sunday, for example, the couple rostered on 'Family Fun' brought two wheelbarrows and we had wheelbarrow races in the hall with the driver blindfolded. One family laid the communion table with homemade bread and port wine. Three teenagers led the service. Kids had a drink and biscuit break halfway through the one-hour service. We had some fun with the reading involving the audience in a sort of chant at predetermined places in the text. The preacher illustrated his message with newspaper clippings stuck on the wall. We have no lectern and the preacher is just as likely to sit and preach in the form of a yarn. Fifteen minutes is maximum for speaking or singing. We have very few musicians so we often sing along to CDs played through our ample sound system. No two services are the same but all finish with a potluck morning tea.

Our Friday night services are more of an adult thing although the whole family comes and has a take-away dinner together. The service is generally quiet, meditative and usually a communion service. We hold this service at our youth outreach centre called FREED'EM HQ. The younger kids play together in an unstructured way. They are welcome to join in the service in the next room if they want, some do, some don't, some wander in and out. The arts feature in this service. We try to incorporate dance, visual displays, story, imagery, candles and incense, etc. There is usually opportunity for personal ministry, which is seldom on offer on Sundays. The music is often quite different, sometimes loud techno other times spooky stuff. Sometimes we sing.

FREED'EM HQ is a community centre for teenagers. Eighty per cent of this group do not go to church and have only scant, if any, knowledge of Jesus. Friday night FREED'EM worship is not only a hit with our church community but it meets the spiritual needs of the teenagers. Our communion table is open to all and we have made it policy to never rush it. One of my greatest joys in ministry is seeing unchurched teenagers kneeling with head buried deep in hands at the table, made of beer crates, sharing The Meal with the rest of us on their turf. FREED'EM worship offers time to reflect and pray with little interruption.

Most of the above information is likely to be out of date by the end of the month. Which month? Every month.

Simon Brown
Email: freedem@ihug.co.nz

The Late Late Service (Glasgow, Scotland)

The Late Late Service is an ecumenical Christian community based in Glasgow committed to expressing and sharing our faith through creative ritual, physical spirituality and authentic worship.

The LLS had its origins at the beginning of the '90s. Andy Thornton who was then the Youth Officer for the Church of Scotland was asked to lead the Youth Night at the General Assembly. Inspired in part by the Nine O'Clock Service in Sheffield, a group got together and created a service that attempted to be relevant and accessible to people of a younger generation. Dance music, video technology, freedom of movement and no 'front' or single person leading the worship, were all elements incorporated into the service.

The group was sufficiently enthused by the creative energy it found in organizing this worship that they decided to continue, and started putting together monthly worship. Initially this was held in a nightclub, but it became clear that those attending were more interested in worship than in being in a club.

Production groups were established when it became unwieldy to create monthly services jointly, and as more people saw the LLS as their only church, there was a need to develop different aspects of church life. A rota of weekly services evolved. A Quiet Service began which was a more contemplative service. It still used a wide variety of visuals (slides and video) and music but tended to be more reflective and introspective than the 'up' Celebration as the dance service came to be called. There was also a Teaching night (which was sometimes led by outside 'experts') and a Personal Growth night which was for members only and which was used to explore our faith in a more intimate or safe environment.

The emphasis was still upon creativity, experimentation and cooperation: instead of being focused mainly on 'artistic excellence' in worship, there was a growing sense of participation, and ways were sought to nurture the gifts and talents of members, to include everyone in service preparation. Rotas of smaller groups were formed to take turns in creating worship.

GROWTH

This was a time of expansion for the Late Late Service. By 1995 it had about 50 members and looked as if it were going to get bigger yet. The LLS had led the mainstage worship at Greenbelt several times, produced services for Radio One (The main UK 'youth' radio station) and Channel 4 Television, attended an alternative worship conference, and were invited to lead more services than the group could manage to cover. Changes were made to the structure of the LLS to help facilitate services and the growing sense of community. Facilitators were put in place to keep an eye on different areas such as music, visuals, education and so on.

THE DEMISE OF THE CELEBRATION

But events (or the Spirit) conspired to take us in a very different direction. Quite a few members moved away from Glasgow (mostly due to career opportunities elsewhere) and suddenly instead of 50 and growing we were 30 and not getting any bigger. Other changes were also taking place: whilst our adult membership had dropped, efforts had been made to build up numbers in other ways, at the end of 1999 the LLS has nineteen children involved with the service and at least a dozen are under the age of six.

All this led us to an extended period of re-evaluation. The Celebration service with its emphasis on technology and high production values was proving exhausting to put on every month, while the 'clubbing' style of service for many (though by no means all) no longer seemed to be 'hitting the spot'. And with so many members now parents, it seemed that a change of style or emphasis was required. The LLS is now embarking on a new kind of worship for us: all age worship, which will include the children as equal members in our worship. The first service is due to take place this month.

The Quiet Service remains our main act of public worship together, and hasn't changed dramatically in style since it first began. But we still have an event every Sunday, a community night for prayer and other meetings for service preparation. A low maintenance event which is nonetheless very important to us is our communion lunch. This grew out of a Good Friday event where the service began with a Middle Eastern style supper laid out in the shape of a cross on the floor – we ate an actual, real meal and then declared that bread and that wine the body and blood of Christ. A bit of research revealed that many of the early Christian images were, not to do with the resurrection but to do with eating scenes – groups eating together in a typical common meal. So we decided to make this a regular event, to dispense with tokens of bread and wine, and have a hearty meal together, which would include a short Eucharist liturgy.

THE FUTURE?

Over the decade that the LLS has been around the sense of community has grown and strengthened. At times we've had to struggle hard to maintain a fully democratic structure with a shared sense of responsibility, but over the last few years the tendency has been to 'deformalize' our structures and to try not to remain fixed in one way of doing things. The LLS can be seen as an example of non-linear cooperation, where there is a balance or tension between integration and self-assertion. The resulting community is therefore not static, but full of dynamic and creative interplay, which makes the whole thing flexible and very open to change. It is true that the 'organic' model can appear very messy, ad hoc, amateurish and downright chaotic; however, it is also true that consensus is the usual result. This year we dropped many 'official' roles (the facilitators) and opted for a more informal 'system of favours' to keep things running, although there is still a steering group that acts as a focus for organization.

At times we have been discouraged, but we always come back to the question "If not this, then what?" Few of us can imagine going back full-time to a mainstream church. Ten years on, the fireworks of alternative worship seem to have settled down to the more permanent glow of a community centred around a creative and collective approach to Christian worship.

Triona Miller

Soul Outpost (Dunedin, New Zealand)

In June of 1997, Mark and Carolyn Kelly-Johnston sent out an exploratory letter to people they thought might be interested. In it they expressed their heartfelt frustration at much of church life:

> We can't enter into worship on Sunday and embark on a pedestrian wade through a four-hymn sandwich without setting aside the 'holy' experience of a bar we spent last night in, listening to a funky soul singer, and sipping Irish coffee. We find worship an unconnected experience when we realise how alien it seems to recall the spiritual energy and gospel motifs we found in the latest version of Romeo and Juliet at the movies. And we often want to cringe in church when we sing a melodic jingle about loving Jesus, when we think of our souls soaring as we play U2's complex 'Pop' album loud on our CD player at home.

Their missive found a response in the hearts of a small group of people, including Mike Riddell, who had recently moved from Parallel Universe in Auckland to the city of Dunedin in the south of New Zealand. Here a handful of Christian fringe-dwellers gathered, and Soul Outpost was born. Using the byline of 'Worship on the Far Side', the fledgling community saw itself exploring new ways of giving expression to faith. From the beginning, there were a wide range of denominational backgrounds represented in the planning group, and the participants decided to maintain a broad and inclusive venture without any institutional links.

Early services took place in a student recreation building, and included such themes as 'If God Will Send His Angels' and 'Home Grown – Kiwi Spirituality'. Each time we would take a theme and go back to basics, asking ourselves 'How can we find the meaning of this for ourselves, and make a response from it to God?' It was exhilarating to be able to use good music and choose video and slide images which played with the theme. We got into the habit of providing coffee and cake, and mulled wine over the winter months (and a roaring fire), which helped people to relax and stay around after the worship. And after every one, when all the gear had been carted out, we were left zinging with excitement.

In early 1998, another member of Parallel Universe's planning team, Jen Long, moved to Dunedin, to strengthen Soul Outpost. Mark and Carolyn had been appointed to a ministry position in another city, but Peter and Agnes Oliver, who had been with Soul Outpost from the beginning, began to play a key role in coordination. The group has always functioned as a community, with no defined roles, and tasks spread according to interest. Over time the shape of the planning group (which is open to anyone) has been fluid as people have moved in and out. As to resources, there was little money to begin with, and that has not changed markedly. But there has always been plenty of enthusiasm and fun.

By now we are on to our third venue. The first suddenly decided that we couldn't use candles there any more, which was too much of a restriction for us to live with. The second was never ideal; an odd-shaped room which made it hard to arrange screens. Now we meet in the back bar of a pub, not far from the university. It has a video projector built in, a sound system, and comes free as long as we buy our drinks from the bar! Our services aim to be monthly, but often it's six weeks before we get the next one together. We decided a long time ago not to put undue pressure on ourselves, and that it needed to be enjoyable for us if we were going to sustain it. There is a mailing list for keeping people in touch with when and where the next event is to be held.

Over the years we have covered a wide range of themes and styles in our worship, from labyrinths to concerts for local musicians to an autumn reflection on 'necessary transitions'. Last week we offered an exploration of spirituality in the city, called 'Urban Vessels' (as in 'We have our treasure in …'). For the upcoming gathering, we'll simply meet in the pub around the fire and have a discussion about a topic of interest. That will take a bit of pressure off us, and help to build the community of people who have come to associate themselves with Soul Outpost. While our group is relatively small (around 30 on a typical night), we have over 100 on the mailing list who turn up sporadically, and for whom Soul Outpost is a sign of hope.

Recently we took over the Dunedin Community Art Gallery for a week, and ran an exhibition during Holy Week entitled 'Images of Easter'. The gallery has a superb location, with large plate glass window opening onto the main street of the city. We invited local artists to contribute work around the theme, and ended up with a mix of paintings, sculpture, video and installation art. Over the few days it was open, we had more than seven hundred people through, many of whom made it their Easter meditation. On the evening of Maundy Thursday, we held our worship (a reflection using Gavin Bryar's 'Jesus Blood Never Failed Me Yet') in the gallery. It was fantastic to be responding to God in the midst of so much creative expression.

Soul Outpost is neither changing the world nor pointing the way forward for the church. It is what it says it is on promotional posters: 'A bunch of people seeking to do spirituality and worship in new ways.' Primarily it's a means of survival for the Christian people within it. Along the way we have collected some very interesting travelling companions, including a New Age meditation group who find a sense of connection with what we're doing. For us and for many of the people who constitute our community, it is a sign of hope that there are new ways of living with God in the contemporary world.

homepages.ihug.co.nz/~mriddell/Soul.html

Introducing Alternative Worship to a Parish Church: A Case Study (Buckingham, UK)

The point of writing this is to encourage people who want to be more creative in their worship, but whose church has never seen anything more alternative than the Anglican Service Book.

BACKGROUND

Having been involved in an alt.worship group for several years (Paradox/Visions, York), we moved house, and started attending a moderately large parish church in a small market town (Buckingham). The leadership got enthused when we described some of the things we'd been doing with worship in York. After loaning them some videos of recent TV programmes of alt.worship, to surface any concerns there might be as early as possible, we were asked if we would do something creative in their church. The local churches ran ecumenical services during Lent, and we were offered the Good Friday evening service.

GETTING AS MANY PEOPLE INVOLVED AS POSSIBLE

It was important that this didn't turn into a two-person show (us). We made regular announcements about the first planning meeting, and had encouragement from some people in the congregation. However, the only ones to show up to plan the service were the vicar and his wife, and one of the lay preachers. It's likely that most just didn't seem to consider that they were equipped to plan services – that's what professional clergy do. However, as the service got nearer, volunteers came forward to play instruments, lead Taizé chants (including a solo), take part in dramatic readings, and operate OHPs and projectors.

'ALT.WORSHIP' FOR THE 40-90S ...?

This was the tricky bit – most of the church congregations who would be attending were aged 40 on, with a smattering of mid-30s. Opening the service at 120bpm was not deemed helpful. We decided that given that it was Good Friday, this should be a meditative service, a journey through darkness into light, following Christ's last seven sayings on the cross.

Once we had a general mood and theme in mind, we found that the same principles that have worked in many different services and groups applied:

Change the space: luckily no pews, so we rearranged the chairs into a circle in the middle of the church, with prayer cushions on the floor in the inner circle, focused on a low altar table (folded trestle table). Together with incense, and low lighting this made the space much more intimate.

Change the lighting: schedule the service for 8–9pm (instead of the usual 6pm); turn the overhead lights off, and use back and front lights only, plus lots of candles.

Change the visual environment: we hung triangular sheets (had to make them) between the side pillars and projected onto the backs of these from the window alcoves. The images changed twice on each screen as the service progressed, from darkness (e.g. Turin shroud; crucifix icons; suffering planet; baby with crown of thorns), to transition (e.g. lighting), to new life (e.g. dove; sunflowers). We projected a large Celtic 'knot-carpet' from the balcony down onto the floor, completely covering the congregation.

The vicar's wife is very artistic, and, together with another couple in the congregation who were good at calligraphy and art, produced stunning prayer stations – some words of Christ on the cross (e.g. "Father forgive them, they don't know what they're doing") illustrated in some way (newspaper headlines and images of suffering); "Father, I place my life in your hands", with photos of babies and patients on life-support machines; "I thirst", on a painted background of a cracked desert. Some of these were metaphors for darkness, others for the turning point, and the others for hope and new life. The visual image of the service was also changed by distributing flyers to local churches and around town, which made it clear that this would be a different service to normal.

Change the power relationships: Jackie led throughout, speaking quietly into a mike while seated on a floor cushion. All readings were by three volunteers sitting within the congregation but with mikes. There was no teaching from the front, but instead the congregation drew their own conclusions and prayers from their visits to the 'prayer stations' we set up at the back and front of the church.

Change the music: Easter liturgical chants, Taize chants (with live music and solo), classical music, Iona, a rock and a dance track, with readings and news samples overlaid (pre-recorded, not by us).

FINDING RESOURCES

Starting from total scratch, we begged without shame. God provided. A local school teacher caught the vision and borrowed several high quality projectors;

others dug theirs out of the attic and loaned them. We made sheeting into triangular screens. We borrowed a portable PA system from some new workmates. Candles, cardboard for the prayer stations and incense was provided by the vicar and wife. Slides provided by Warehouse, our previous group. Music from our own collection. Power extension cables we had to buy. OHPs and screens provided by other churches.

We had about seven weeks from agreeing to do it, to the service night. About one night a week was spent for the first few weeks planning. This increased steadily, and two weeks before, a week that we'd booked for holiday turned into more or less full-time service preparation! In other words, if you're not taking time off, you may need two months to prepare for the first service, there's so much infrastructure to lay! Set-up began at 3.30pm, after another service (sound familiar?!). We had made sure there were sufficient bodies (about seven) to do the work of hanging screens, moving chairs, etc.

THE RESULT

We had more people than anyone expected (about 100). With a few exceptions (and one unfortunate woman who about-heeled as soon as she smelled the incense – she was asthmatic!), people have told us they were inspired by the service, and want to know when the next one is! (Oh yes, there was also the old lady who told the vicar she wouldn't be coming on principle, since it wasn't right to be having a slide show on Good Friday.) Several said that they were stunned by how the familiar old space had been transformed by creating a circle. Others have said that they had long wanted to see worship move forward, but didn't want happy-clappy choruses, which was the only alternative they knew of.

NOW WHAT?

Following this initial effort, which by any measure was extremely encouraging, the church now faces the next step. We are in the interesting position of needing to help resource the people to continue this themselves, because (1) we're only attending the church as a temporary measure while we house-sell and hunt, and (2) they need to begin to own it more themselves. We managed to create a service for folks a generation ahead of us, and managed through being able to envision how a service could go, and having learned a load of practical techniques from other services.

Being able to imagine how things can be different is the key – many of us may have forgotten just how powerful and exciting it can be to walk into an alt.service environment for the first time – it really blows you away. Now that people here have seen what's possible, we have to hope that the seeds of creativity, fanned by the Spirit, will start to flourish in lots of different people, as they begin to figure out how to develop their own worship, and make it accessible to the local community. Our role, we think, is to help out for as long as we're around, but the service planning group for the next service ("Vicar: How about Pentecost?…") is going to have to be a lot bigger! – and we think it will be.

POSTSCRIPT – ONE YEAR ON

Following that service, enthusiasm was such that they wanted to do another. With more people participating in the planning this time, we did a harvest evening service, which was extremely creative – outrageous even – with real smelly rubbish piles, skeletons, guns, barbed wire etc. on one side of the church (the 'field of deprivation') and a veritable western, bountiful harvest paradise on the other side ('field of blessing'). The people were placed in the middle and at various points in the service given time and space to visit these, and then 'do what comes naturally to you; meditate; act; pray'. They spontaneously cleaned up the rubbish, watered the dry plants, and shared out the fruit and flowers.

We then unveiled screened-off areas of the poor and rich side, which had the 'shadow' that is so often forgotten: we discovered the richness of community, wisdom, and art in the 'poor world' that we miss so much; in our 'advanced nations', the cost of Western lifestyle in crime, community breakdown, mental health, etc. – just in case they were planning on leaving with the concept that We're rich and They're poor. It was tremendously exciting. Our goal was to facilitate them to construct and own their own meaning/significance from this environment, and we felt that a step was taken towards this.

We've since left that church having moved house, but they are continuing to do creative services, albeit on a lower key due to lack of resources. One of the most 'radical' things that we did as newcomers was rearrange the seats (breaking a spell of several hundred years). This changes the space so drastically, and has since been adopted as common practice in their monthly special child-oriented family service (although it's apparently not considered appropriate for grown-ups yet …).

Jackie and Simon Buckingham Shum
Email: S.Buckingham.Shum@open.ac.uk

Visions

Our community in York started in 1989 when a group of people met together to plan a Christian arts and music venue that would be using a disused warehouse for a month as part of the events surrounding a mission in York Minster. The group, then known as "Warehouse", was born. Many people from different churches were involved in this event. Yet when the excitement of the initial project was over, a smaller group of us continued to meet together. Our aim was to explore community, the arts, and mission within a postmodern culture.

We wanted, eventually, to have a venue similar to the original Warehouse, to be a Christian arts and music venue, but we also wanted to be able to start a late night multimedia service, similar to the events that were happening in Sheffield at that time. We attached ourselves, for pastoral support, to the church of St Michael-le-Belfrey, which had been famous in the 1970s for pioneering new and exciting ways of utilizing art, music and drama within worship. Graham Cray, our vicar at the time, was particularly helpful and supportive, encouraging us in our efforts to find artistic ways of expressing our worship that would be appropriate to the young adult subcultures within York.

In August 1991 we had the first "Warehouse" Anglican multimedia church service. It was initially an experiment, to which we invited many people older and wiser than ourselves, (including the Bishop of Selby) to give comments, help and advice. We then officially opened our church doors to the public in March 1992.

Our initial service was a dance-based teaching service, with half an hour of sung worship, which was performed over dance tracks we had written ourselves. This was followed by a time of teaching, which was little different to a standard church sermon. This service happened once a month. Over time we gradually realized that this approach wasn't very effective within a culture that is so visual and experiential in nature. We experimented, becoming more visual in our teaching; using video and word loops as part of a service which became more integrated in its approach to the subject being presented whilst still being relevant to dance music and club culture.

We have often been invited to produce artwork, slides and video for secular club nights in the York area, and more recently we have become involved in a project to launch a Christian multimedia ambient café venue in York. The rise of late night café culture in the last couple of years has particularly interested us. The intimacy of a cafe venue lends itself to deep conversations in a way that nightclubs do not. Our vision is for a café venue where several different types of good coffee and snacks are served, excellent ambient music is played (sometimes live) and the visual art is exciting and innovative. But also where there is always someone available to listen to people's problems, to pray for them if they wish, to offer practical help if appropriate, or just to offer a shoulder to cry on.

A couple of years after we began our dance service we started our communion service. The communion now takes place on the first Sunday of the month and the dance service on the third Sunday of the month. The communion is more meditative in style, using gentle ambient synthesizer music throughout. This is where we began our first experiments in integrating more experimental and practical forms of prayer. We soon discovered just how powerful these were, both as a way of communicating with God and as a way of discovering more about ourselves. We were inspired by other groups throughout our country doing similar things with their worship and integrated some of their ideas into our worship. We also changed our name from Warehouse to Visions to reflect our multimedia nature and also our desire to have dreams and visions about the shape of the church of the future.

Nowadays Visions meet together on three Sundays a month. As well as the dance and communion services, we meet on the second Sunday of the month for prayer and use a medieval labyrinth, candles, plainchant music and Bibles to aid us in our prayer. We also have a midweek small group where we meet to explore and discuss our faith together.

We are just one of the many experimental services that have sprung up around the world in recent years. Stylistically these alternative worship services are very varied, yet one thing all these new congregations seem to have in common is a desire for worship to become more participatory. They are inspiring others to become less like consumers and to take a more active part in the planning and execution of their worship meetings. For art as part of worship is not an elitist thing. It is a tool we can all use to enrich our prayer lives and enhance our devotions, enabling us to express our love for God in new ways.

Sue Malcolm
www.abbess.demon.co.uk/paradox/

Like everything which starts out new, the alternative worship movement has had its share of problems. One of the most dramatic events in the network of emergent groups was the collapse of the Nine O'clock Service in August of 1996, with newspaper headlines revealing a pattern of sexual abuse in what was portrayed as a weird Anglican cult. It came as a huge unwelcome shock to people engaged in new worship, and served as a painful reminder that trying new things doesn't automatically protect people from some very old temptations. To those in the alt.worship community, the sobering thought arose that it might be the loosening of traditional boundaries which made us all more susceptible to disaster. And yet that danger has not been sufficient to persuade many of those involved in new ventures to cease and desist.

Alternative worship groups have been around long enough now to encounter issues which are specific to what they're trying to do. It's not until you've been on the road for a while that some of these issues become apparent. In highlighting some of them here, we're trying to do two things. The first is to deflate the idea that what we're talking about is a new 'movement' which will save the

> We are of a highly literate culture. We expect to be able to make choices, to investigate and to critique. I am not an eleventh-century serf relying on my priest and my prince to make my spiritual and economic decisions for me (risking hell or hanging if, in my ignorance, I dissent).
>
> Andrew

church overnight, and whisk all its troubles away. And secondly, we want to share what we think are the growing edges and hazards, in the hope that it might help to prevent us all from making the same mistakes. Furthermore, if we're going to keep alive the hope that the church can be reformed for this new millennium, then we need to share whatever learnings we have with each other along the way. The following, then, are a few thoughts to stimulate the ongoing conversation.

Relevance vs Trendiness

The incarnation itself gives us the model of relevance. God shows up on our turf, speaking our language so that we might understand. It seems that the love of God is continually streaming outwards and finding new expression in order that it might be made apparent to people. Maggi Dawn, in her article in *The Post-Evangelical Debate,* makes the point strongly that relevance involves almost constant willingness to reshape the tradition, given the rapidly changing nature of our current context. If we neglect that reshaping, we end up preserving a gospel which says something quite different from what we intend it to say. So it is that a message which Christians claim is liberating and inclusive ends up being perceived by many in our culture as bigoted and repressive.

> I don't want to 'understand' and feel secure because I have a rationale for the way I relate to God in a culturally hip manner. I want to face the shifting cultural values, and free my perspective of God from being limited to one, static, antiquated system of worship.
>
> Lu

On the other hand, however, we need to remember the adage that those who are wedded to the fashion of the day will end up widowed tomorrow. If relevance is for its own sake, we risk both breaking faith with our tradition, and appearing stupid to those around us. It's very easy to fall into what we sometimes talk about as the 'trendy vicar' syndrome. You know the scenario; a village vicar is shown on television wearing a leather jacket and playing guitar in church, in order to attract young people. The saddest part is that the whole thing is a send-up by the media, and the vicar doesn't even realize the fact. Relevance can never be simply stylistic; nor is it something that can be imitated from the outside. The only genuine way of being relevant is to inhabit the same world as those you are working among, and this is a deeper enterprise than getting a different haircut.

New worship at times runs the risk of trespassing into trendiness. I have been responsible for planning some worship which I look back and cringe at. It ended up being crass and patronizing. There are two underlying issues in saving us from the trendy vicar syndrome. The first is the recognition that we always live in the force-field between relevance and identity. We can only ever be relevant as Christians if we are firmly rooted in our tradition. Our identity as the people of Christ must be understood, affirmed, reflected upon and confessed. To lose our grip on that heritage is always an act of betrayal, and ends not in relevance but apostasy. Secondly, we need to be thoroughly immersed in our surrounding cultures, and not kept apart from them by Christian sub-culture. Only when we inhabit culture will we be able to pick up the subtle nuances of it which allow us to make connections between our faith and our context.

By the People or For the People?

A fundamental commitment of most alternative worship groups is to the participation and inclusion of people. There's a desire to get away from a 'front' and a group of leaders who perform worship on behalf of everyone else, with a passive audience consuming it all. If some sort of response to God on the part of everyone present has not been facilitated, then something has gone wrong in the process. In the course of finding different means of achieving this, a lot of groups have tried a variety of ways of going about it. Communion of some sort is never far from the centre; discussion in small clusters is common; dancing is a means of involvement in many UK groups; contemporary prayers and liturgy are often responsive; and frequently people are encouraged to participate in rituals of some kind.

However, the very nature of the worship sometimes makes it seem like a spectator activity. The use of big images, video and pumping sound creates a certain frisson of excitement, but it can also be isolating and overpowering. It's easy for people to get lost in the midst of it; to withdraw into individuality and a world of private experience rather than shared response. And all of the technology is being driven by a small group of people hovering over control panels. Is it worship, or is it a show which is being put on? Inevitably, some of the strongest elements of the worship are planned by a few on behalf of the others, and therefore run the risk of being imposed on people rather than being generated by them. How then is this different from more traditional modes of worship?

To avoid replicating the mistakes of the past, it is vital that we find meaningful ways of allowing people to participate at every level of our worship. Unless it is 'the work of the people', it will be deficient in some way. On the other hand, there will always be delegated roles within worship. Though it is exhilarating to try from time to time, getting all those assembled to plan worship on the spot is limiting and can be confusing. Generally, it's necessary to have a group to plan the outlines of each event. Such groups can and should be as open as possible, and can easily rotate between events, but the process which the particular collection of planners go through in preparation for worship is as important as the end result. In a healthy community, there will be a high degree of trust in other members to take on responsibility for certain tasks on behalf of others.

That said, there is a lot of learning to be done in this area. At the risk of generalizing in a stereotypical manner, there is often something about the way that men plan worship which produces a greater emphasis on technology and less on inclusion, whereas women may value participation above production. It needs to be emphasised again that alternative worship is not about technology, but about bringing our shared experience as a response to God. From walking a labyrinth, to planting seeds in soil as a sign of hope, to scrawling on a graffiti prayer wall, there are many low-tech options for the involvement of people in worship. The provision of options for people, including that of opting out, is an act of inclusion and embrace which speaks of the gospel.

Conversion

Some people of a certain evangelical persuasion just can't help themselves. They always want to know how many converts there have been; the universal litmus test of whether any movement, church or activity is 'of God'. Those of us in the alternative worship movement begin to get a bit vague and mumbly in the face of such interrogation, if not downright defensive. As it happens, people have come to faith through new worship, and sometimes significant numbers. But the way it happens looks so different from anything which our church background leads us to expect, that we become reluctant to distort the picture by accepting misleading words. Nor are many of us happy to have our endeavours evaluated in terms of one category. The whole trend towards 'results' is part of what we are reacting against.

We talk much more about 'journey' than 'conversion'. Journey toward Christ and journey away from Christ. It is not easy from the outside to identify which way a person is travelling. Many with religious language seem to be moving away from Jesus, just as others with no words to express their feelings seem to be reaching out for him. There is a missiological dimension which is never far from worship. When the presence of God is celebrated by people, and that celebration is accessible, then God becomes newly recognizable by those who may not quite have 'seen' before. But worship can never be used as 'a means to an end' without debasing it. Friends who see an older couple deeply in love may be warmed by it; but the love between the pair is not 'employed' to benefit onlookers.

We have discovered that people are coming to faith differently than they did a generation or so ago. At one time it seemed that people needed to be persuaded of the 'truth' of the gospel, so that they believed and subsequently joined up with a church. Now it is much more common for someone to find a place among a group of friendly people, and hang out with them for a while before raising any questions of 'belief'. The phrase that is often used in alternative worship circles is that 'belonging precedes believing'. It is much more often the pattern that faith is eased into sometime after participation. Often the 'decision point' is difficult to locate, though it is always good to mark one through a definitive event like baptism.

Re-reading the story of Jesus has been helpful in connecting our new experience with the heritage of faith. In the Gospels, it seems that Jesus calls people to join with him and follow his pilgrimage into the unknown. He doesn't ask them many questions, and most of them don't even begin to understand what the movement is about until they've been on the road for some time. Along the way, the followers either position themselves closer to Jesus, or quietly drop by the wayside. This is a good analogy for the process observed among emergent Christian groups.

> This desperate evangelical need to save the flock and spread the word makes about as much sense as handing out leaflets to explain gravity, or explaining why the sky is blue. What's important is what you're going to do today beneath this clear blue sky. Who you'll meet, what you'll create.
>
> Willie

Building Faith

All of which raises the question of how people might be welcomed into and educated in the Christian faith. Alt.worship groups are generally started by people who have had at least some experience of the mainstream Church and for whatever reason no longer feel comfortable within that framework. Their life is built around contrasts – *not* doing things the way they used to be done. At its worst this can be negative and reactionary but at its best it is deeply effective and gives rise to significant new ways of approaching Christian faith and worship. The group experiences God in refreshingly meaningful ways and the journey becomes one of ever widening vistas and new experiences. Worship that is a real alternative.

But what about the person who comes from the outside without the benefit of this past heritage? The person who doesn't have a language and a memory of stories and traditions to reframe and modify and reject? How does this person gain the basics of the faith that will enable them to become a consistent mature follower of Christ?

> Once you torch the family mansion the sense of disorientation is massive. For me to come to terms with a new sense of faith was a far, far bigger conversion experience than 'becoming a Christian'.
>
> Peter

If real alternatives to the mainstream church are to be provided, it is necessary to seriously consider ways of delivering initiation into the basics of the Christian faith. One alt.worship service a month will not be enough. Almost certainly small groups will need to meet at other times in order to take care of this basic catechetical need, or new ways of teaching will need to be developed. It cannot be assumed that everyone who comes in is at the same level of understanding or maturity. In the end, there is no substitute for the sort of relationship-based model of passing on learnings and stories. This requires time and commitment on the part of the experienced follower of Jesus.

One healthy new development has been the number of ordinary people undertaking some form of theological education. Such students have no intention of any formal 'ministry', but find that picking up a few basic papers of a theological degree or diploma provides a disciplined and helpful introduction to the mysteries of Christian faith. With more and more of such courses becoming web-based, they begin to be more accessible and practical for those who have limited time available.

Going it Alone

Most of what has been said so far concerns several people getting together to produce worship as a way of moving forward on their Christian journey. What about those who for reasons of practicality or choice want to maintain their Christian spirituality and faith journey alone? The following reflection comes from one such:

> Speaking as one who, at best, might be described as being on the fringes of the church (though even this would grossly overstate my actual involvement therein) ... despite many years of effort in teens/20s, "church" hasn't ever worked for me, but my chosen career eventually ended any notions of being a regular attendee of anything. Hence, early struggles of guilt vs. boredom, as to whether to persevere with this Ancient Institution were neatly solved by my nomadic existence.
>
> On my journey, the more distance I gained between myself and my church roots, the less able I became to comprehend that this institution, en masse, could be worth propping up.

Not with any malice or bitterness, but just through observation and getting on with life. It confused me that so many bright people would spend so much time dealing with the centuries of associated baggage; defending the institutional inevitabilities which you can't possibly believe in or think are good ideas.

For those who feel this way or find themselves in a similar position, what exists to help sustain Christian spirituality? It might be helpful to start with a read of Dave Tomlinson's *The Post-evangelical*, a reminder that experiencing such feelings does not place people outside the fold. His book also lists some materials on faith development that would be helpful. *Finding Faith: A Self Discovery Guide for Your Spiritual Quest* by Brian McLaren is also worthwhile. Most of Mike Riddell's books are written for people outside the Christian faith or struggling with it and their themes and approach might prove sustaining.

Ultimately it can be very difficult to pursue the Christian journey totally alone. The fact is that the Christian faith is about community. It is only in the presence of other believers that much of the Jesus story makes sense and is able to be appropriated.

Children

The old adage that 'children crying in church are like good intentions – they should always be carried out' is not a helpful perspective. Children have a vital place in the life of a worshipping congregation. The problem is figuring out where that place is.

Glenbrook Community Church, Graceway and The Late Late Service, whose stories are on the CD-ROM (in 'Hopeful Rumours'), describe some of the struggles and successes these groups have had involving children in worship. Any group that is together for more than a few years will face this issue. The tension is between involving children in meaningful ways and yet not pitching the service entirely at their level. Most alternative worship groups are keen to involve children in the 'main' worship and not banish them to do their own separate thing. This is an easier belief to hold than it is to practise. On the other hand, there is much about new worship that is child-friendly. It is participative, image-based, creative, interactive and sometimes loud. Groups such as Soul Outpost have discovered that children become keenly involved in the worship, and look forward to the next event, even when they feel bored and excluded by conventional church services.

> I think I have grown a fairly self-contained faith, which isn't necessarily influenced by external factors like the quality of church life, the theology in whatever book I have just read or the teaching delivered by the clergy person. Something that has really made a difference is knowing others who walk a different path but who have had similar feelings and longings. I will always need the company of others, the space to enjoy them and the freedom to tell of my encounters with God.
>
> Jemima

Happy Families by John and Olive Drane (London: Marshall Pickering, 1995) doesn't give the answers we might want but it does raise some of the issues to do with families and children and worship.

Alt.Future?

Is alternative worship, such as described in this Project, the future of the church in the West? Who knows? Probably not. Certainly, the church in the West is in serious trouble and likely to run itself into the ground in the next generation if it doesn't do something radical. It's difficult to believe the prophets who say that we are on the edge of a great revival. They promote a Christian spiritual awakening that will fill our churches to the choir seats again.

> My faith is largely based now on what I can do for Jesus … more so than on how much I know about the Bible or how often I pray or whether I go to church. I decided somewhere in the last 18 months that my faith was out there in the community as much as it is in me.
>
> Jo

God is active in the world (perhaps more so than in the church) and the world is more spiritually aware than it has been for a very long time. Perhaps God is going to do a re-creation job on the church rather than a re-formation. It appears that the future church will look radically different to the present church, and that new models of doing church will be needed during the current period of transition. No one model will be right or best. This is not a time of master plans or franchised churches. It is a time of groups who grapple with issues of the emerging culture and the living out of their faith as followers of Jesus in that culture. This multiplicity of new models, their failures and their successes, their evolution and their demise will be what funds the movement of God into the future. One model among many. The church must become all things to all people so that by all means some might become followers of Christ.

Abuse

Adopting new music and words does not save any community from the predilection to sinfulness. The history of the church teaches us that the followers of Christ succumb to recurrent problems when it comes to issues like power and control. Abuse could almost be catalogued as one of the 'marks' of the church. To a certain extent, the current disenchantment with church in the Western world is a product of former abuses. Sexual abuse, abuse of power and spiritual abuse are all demonstrably evident in the established church. And, tragically, they have already emerged among groups associated with new worship. In some ways the new groups are more vulnerable than the institutional church. In the latter, bitter experience has led to the creation of certain safeguards (at least against non-institutional abuse); whereas the desire of emergent groups for loose structure and accountability provides scope for disaster.

Hopefully it will be possible to limit the predilection toward abuse in the new groups without introducing the entire legislative programme which weighs so heavily in the established church. The necessary protective qualities include transparency, collective accountability, shared decision-making, inclusive leadership, mutual trust and a healthy cynicism. The dream of most emergent communities is that the fostering of such qualities will help to limit the appalling damage which is caused by ecclesiastical abuse. Already chastened by their first encounter with such tragedy, new worshipping groups are at least more aware now of the dark possibilities which may never entirely be banished from the realms of possibility.

The Story of Alternative Worship in Two Versions (Cynical and Optimistic)

The text of a talk given by Andy Thornton at the Alternative Worship Gathering in London, 9 May 1998.

This is the story of alternative worship written in two versions, firstly the cynical version and secondly the optimistic version. Guaranteed to offend *and* flatter. So let us begin with the cynical version.

CYNICAL VERSION

Once upon a time, there was a group of people. The characteristic of this group was firstly that they were over-inducted theologically. Each had spent too long in their bedrooms talking with people holding similar views to them and coming to the same conclusion; they were right and the rest of the church was wrong. The comfort of knowing that they were right had been enough to keep them from doing anything spectacular for years. Each was culturally critical and creative, they knew how to understand, they knew how to manipulate, they knew how to make their own piece of culture whether it be songs, videos, art, drama – everything was at their fingertips.   However, it was one thing having it at your fingertips and it was another doing it. This group of people had a saturation of church that had formed their Christian experience. Each had gathered a little too often for their own good, had sought God in meeting after meeting and found God all too occasionally.

However, it was not enough to leave this environment and go to seek God elsewhere. Instead they stayed too long in that environment, harbouring resentment at those who had made it and not letting in the group of knowledgeable ones. What's more, this group had carried a psychologically warped understanding of how the universe operated. This was brought forward from their induction into Christianity as teenagers where God was seen as the root principle above which the whole world operates. The implication of this straightforward understanding of God was that it was continually possible to root out the most true and underlying motivational reality behind everything.

In searching for the one clear answer behind the great problem of why more people were not becoming Christians, they understood that the main problem with Christianity was that church culture was completely out of date and that the barrier to real truth coming out and spilling into the nation was that there was too great a gap between the culture of church and the culture of the life around them.

Then one day, part of this big group of people hidden within the rest of the church broke out. Through a serious of miraculous experiences the door was opened for them to walk forward and do it their own way. And so began the story of alternative worship. Next the very independent, highly critical, power hungry ones started a project to prove their point. The project involved them doing all the things they had wanted to do in order to get rid of the problem of why the church culture was so different from the real world. They lived in community, they prayed powerful prayers, they liberated gifts (particular leadership ones) and they set about making a new church on the principle that the answer had come and that they were it.

And it worked. People were spectacularly drawn to it. They were persuaded of the answer and they were co-opted into the project. What started as a group of twelve soon became a group of one hundred, two hundred, and then four hundred. And around the country others felt empowered to join in on their own terms and in their own places. Drawn forward by the success and the confidence that the answer had come and was being proven to be right. And so slowly out of the woodwork came groups of similar people, each characterized by various similarities: by a faith in God that was holding on by a thread but a hope that it might be revived, in parallel with the hope that their cultural cynicism about church could be vindicated by the success of their project. At last they could put two fingers up at those who had made them feel second-rate because they

> God, Father
> give me strength
> to burst asunder
> this black black
> coffin
> closing on me;
> life
> enough to raise
> your dead dead
> children
> from holy death;
> courage to carry
> the flame
> in the dark dark
> night
> of uncertainty;
> and wisdom
> to cut the cancer
> and not the flesh
> it feeds upon.
>
> Mike

could not tolerate the figure who embodied the great oppression, Graham Kendrick.

There were other characteristics that came to light about these similar-minded people. First, they were boys with toys. Yes, they were men who were psychologically attached to 'doing something for God' by their years of sitting under the evangelical ministry but they were incapable of doing any form of communication that involved them talking one to one, face to face with other people. Instead they needed technological intermediaries to hide behind in order to communicate with the rest of the world. In this way they could control their image, they could control their message and they could mitigate against anyone coming forward and disagreeing with them because the technology was the voice and they were simply standing behind it.

Secondly, they were a group of people starved of ritual. They had lived in very literal ecclesiastical communities and now they needed a less verbal way of saying things. (Particularly when they weren't too sure what they wanted to say any more.) It soon emerged that one of the clear answers to the needs of the world was ritual. This would compensate for the over-dogmatic version of Christianity in which they had previously been power-brokers. (Little did they realize that they had to forgive themselves and disavow their pasts in order to move forward.)

Thirdly, they were cynical of leadership. Principally because they had been better leadership potential than anyone else around them, but they were not going to be leaders themselves as they did not respect the people in their church enough to want to lead them.

Fourthly, they each carried a dissident mentality. They were happier to sit on the sidelines and criticize (and therefore always be right) than to actually do something of which they might be criticized. Once they had started their own thing and it was not working for them, each could move to the edge of their own thing and end up permanently on the outside still feeling right, still harbouring the dissident mentality.

Fifthly, they had an interest in inventiveness. Yes, the new thing had to happen time and time again, years and years of looking for the chance to innovate finally came to the surface. In fact it came so far to the surface that they reached the point when novelty and worship was an indicator of the life of God. If God was doing a new thing then it had to be done in video, slide, music

> Life is like a wave, like a stream, like a journey, like a billion-and-one clichés that weren't always clichés, but became them because we cannot possibly hope to bottle the mystery and sell it for $99.95 with a beautiful day-glo label and fresh alpine scent ...
>
> Rick

and ritual. The domain of God became synonymous with the domain of worship.

And sixthly, they had discovered the power of reflection in their own lives. Not only did they not have enough ritual but they also did not have enough space in worship in order to simply sit together and reflect on their experience of the week. Little did they realize that this emphasis on reflection would soon become a safe haven for never having to declare anything about their faith. So what started off as a new way to make their journey ended up in a cul-de-sac of reflection and being left to think on their own in an already over-individualistic world (sufficiently late-90s to leave no-one challenged but everyone included).

But the church adopted the new groups because they saw the big model working. Yes, the group that started with twelve was now five hundred, six hundred. It was jumping, it was lively although it was somewhat secretive as to how it achieved all its ends. It was nevertheless the great answer to the great new word, 'postmodern'. Although some had grave doubts about how things were going at the heart of the big group, it seemed to be ever moving into new territory – a vanguard movement on a messianic mission to reform and to remake the church for the new millennium. It had new language and even brought in new gurus to enable its double exodus to leave church and to leave the world and become the new place of security for the truly spiritual.

> This generation is facing the stock-market crash of organized religion, and much as it's encouraging to see my friends taking this on board and moving early, it worries me that I see in them an accompanying disillusionment or bitterness; their investment having been so much larger than mine ever was.
>
> Peter

Until the day the bubble burst. It was discovered that the group was founded on coercion and manipulation, that the journey was prompted and tainted by a greed for power. And the great hope was gone. The proof that it had all worked vanished. To some degree it began to look like the same old story – all it was, was a new group with a new set of answers chopping itself off from the history of the church. It looked something like the house church but with bass bins, lights and smoke. And the others who were left after this collapse began a period of readjustment. The jubilant dancing stopped. People said it is OK to be small, quality counts. And inward journey was stressed over corporate proclamation. And individualism was revered and the need to respect difference became the bench-mark of quality. And the sense of the corporate, confident missiology diffused because they had believed that the medium was the message but they were too tired and downhearted to keep going with the medium. In fact, if the medium was the message then the message was simple, 'I'm knackered!'

So they went on quietly reflecting and saying, 'now what was the message? Is it something I should tell anyone else? ... ' I hope you have not been too hurt by my cynical version. It is kind of antisocial and also something of the truth. But here is the optimistic version.

OPTIMISTIC VERSION

Once upon a time, in a land not too far from here, there was ... the seventies. And in the seventies, the church discovered a new thing. It woke up to the fact that the culture of Christianity did not really exist. That there was no point in carrying forward the old ecclesiastical ways because they were birthed in a different culture. What they needed to do in this time of great modernity was to re-appropriate the message of the Christian gospel into the new emerging culture. A project had to begin which reformed and remade the culture of church so that there was no gap between the culture of church and the then rock-dominated culture of the time. And all those who came into the church for the first time learnt this lesson.

Part of the message of the new gospel was that it should fit the culture and not come bound and gagged to a previous era's definition of Christian culture. And by the mid-eighties, there were pockets of people who were creative, accomplished and had insight into the changes and culture around them but had never really bought in to the late-sixties culture that had dominated the church in the late seventies. They were powerful because they could critique the culture and the construct of church and also recognize the possibility of options for the worship framework. They were articulate, contemporary and ambitious. And so many of these new people embarked on a series of experiments.

The first thing they recognized that had to change was the environment within which worship happened. No longer would it work to bring people familiar with restful or stimulating environments and put them into the cold and clinical atmosphere of the multi-purpose buildings that were called churches. Something had to happen. It takes a radical change of environment to provoke a radical change of temperament which was needed to shift the over-entertained, over-worked, over-fed and over-easy people of the eighties into a mind set to be ready for the challenge and the mystery of God. And the time was not right either.

Church was happening on a Sunday morning when everyone was in bed. What was needed was a brave new attempt to re-appropriate Christianity for a culture which spent its week's earnings on the Saturday night and its Sunday morning asleep. So the new experiments began late on a Sunday evening when people were in quite a different mood. When the day had been spent relaxing and socialising and when the openness of the individual to a new experience was probably at its height. And there were unspoken rules for the new experiment. First and foremost it should be as close as possible to those who the experiments were designed for. In the late eighties a new culture of dance was emerging which meant that it was possible to perceive a culture amongst the young which was fairly homogeneous and exemplified by the rave, high-energy celebration situation. But over the years new rules began to fund the bedrock of the experiments.

Firstly, that the project of worship should engage the whole person and not just the intellect or just the emotions. This brave new attempt to bring holistic spirituality into the contemporary situation was happening in many of the situations and so groups discovered some similarities to other communities such as the Iona Community and Celtic Christianity. A second rule was that the experiment should be adventurous, should not be compromised by previous church traditions or expectations of those already in the church, but should welcome contemporary culture in a way that did not necessarily have to see it as the equivalent of the biblical phrase, 'the world'. Thirdly, the principle of the experiment should be that it worked 'for me', not for a mythical third person for whom we were doing our experiments. And so the benchmark of a good worship occasion should be that it was meaningful to those who designed and participated in it and not to those who were standing at a distance and being openly critical.

And fourthly, the rule for these groups would be that they should be humble and claim little for themselves. Although things worked in their situation they were not on a mission from God to reform the whole church by their success. They were to have space to be able to fail and space to be able to succeed without being evaluated and held to ransom by the need for numerical success. But some groups were numerically successful. They shied away from sharing too much with the larger church because the principle of their activity was more important than the practice or the media which they used. And in their search for newness, they discovered that the seventies church had made itself much poorer by trying to continually inaugurate Christianity into the culture of its time.

The groups went back into history and found that perhaps five hundred, perhaps a thousand, fifteen hundred, two thousand years ago, there had been men and women of theological and spiritual insight whose works and approaches were excitingly new for the late twentieth century. They found that they were opening a massive storehouse of treasure which was falling out into their lap and being reused to enliven the spirituality of those hungry for the mystery which the soul needs in order to find balance in the life of God. And so the groups reintegrated a whole new wealth of holistic Christian expression.

> Community is something I'm somewhat of a novice at ... but God is surely not. May God allow us this community and this space to wonder and rely and quest forever after Him and share in our discoveries ...
>
> Rick

In the experiments many who were satisfied with the conventional church lost faith with the experimenters. They had seen them starting on a journey which was fulfilling the bounds of acceptability, i.e. moving towards the lost generation with a new way of expressing the gospel, but these groups were doing more than that. They were founding new principles on which the gospel should be re-evaluated for the culture around them. And their language was changing and was no longer fitting in with the language of Zion.

The experiments became a cauldron of new ideas. Networks of experimenters grew and founded new principles of making sense of spirituality. They met together and tried to discern how to engage with new theologies for a new era, the next millennium. Some answers emerged, but as time went on they recognized that they were uncovering bigger and bigger questions which would then become the foundational touchstones for their future journey. They recognized that they had stumbled across something unique in terms of developing a new repertoire of spirituality. That late-twentieth-century people were looking for new exercises by which to engage and arouse the soul out of the torpor caused by consumerism. They introduced people to Christianity by showing them the practices and not the principles. They advocated a soft way in to the faith that was not based around an ultimatum or decision time but a slow induction into a radical series of challenges that came alongside a growing awareness of the spiritual need of the individual.

The only problem facing this group was that their growth was happening alongside an increasingly loud, revival-obsessed right-wing church which was growing in confidence by the minute as it fostered a vision of a nation returning to worship in bigger and bigger stadiums and attracting the business-oriented English career man into a successful church whose proof was in its numbers and whose comfort was in signs and wonders.

The group of experimenters recognized that they must not be thrown off the project or be intimidated from sharing their insights confidently when they found themselves in the context of other louder, more confident more mission-orientated representations of the Christian community. They had to find a new way of communicating a gentle holistic faith where God waits and does not push. They needed new metaphors to understand their journey. They wanted to envisage the kingdom of God as a shopping mall and not a department store – a place where all the treasures of God could be found but where there are many doors into the same treasure trove. They recognized they had a harder project because it is so difficult to sell a package that is not a package in a package-orientated world.

So one weekend they gathered together in London. They said to each other, now where were we? How can we start believing that we are normal enough so that what works for us will work for others? How can we stay confident and build up the mission that has been emerging when around us we find ourselves barricaded by the voice of an ultimatum-driven black-and-white church? How do we give a soft message in a hard culture? How did we arrive here? Can we bear the idea that we're a dying movement? Can we tolerate the consequences of being successful? Does 'successful' mean being permanently on the edge of the mainstream? Who wants to hear what we have to say? And are we ready to tell anyone the results of our experiment as if it should matter to them? ...

> I am mind-bogglingly tired. I do not know what to think. I believe that God himself has a very good idea about what is happening, and what is ahead. I trust, and I am blind. I walk and I wonder where I am going. I know exactly where I am going, and I have no idea how the hell this road is going to get me there. And yet, I believe.
>
> ckp

And a Final Word from Us ...

In writing this book, we have simply been sharing something of our own experiences along the way, as we struggle to make sense of what God's future may bring for all of us. And now we have spoken enough. We have come to a pause but not to an end. The journey we are on may have a destination, but the one thing we're sure of is that we haven't yet reached it. From this vantage point, it appears that our expedition may lead us over the horizon, to a place only imagined. We have called this book a 'project' for good reason; it is ongoing, incomplete and tenuous. You, the readers, will play a part in what happens from here on in. We travel on in hope, making common pilgrimage with whatever nomads we encounter along the way. Perhaps it is a circular trip, like that of the Prodigal this project is named after, and we will arrive eventually not far from where we started. But if that is the case, we will be very different people. And the voyage will have been essential. This one fact we know: our journey is toward Love. What we have left behind is insignificant compared to that which we are approaching. May the wind of the Spirit lead us all to that sheltering place under the wings of God.

RESOURCES

Services, Churches and Groups

The websites of most alternative worship services, in the UK and worldwide, can be found on links from: www.greenbelt.org.uk/altgrps/altg.html or www.churchNet.org.uk/listings.shtml
Alternative Faith Community Network: www.futuresgroup.org.nz
First Church of Cyberspace: www.godweb.org
The Next Level Church (Denver): www.tnl.org
Mars Hill Church (Seattle): www.marshill.org
Pathways Church (Denver): www.pathwayschurch.org
Building the Bridges (Denver): www.buildingthebridges.com

Howard, R. *The Rise and Fall of the Nine O'Clock Service: A Cult within the Church?* London: Mowbray, 1996.

Magazines/Bulletin Boards/General

Ship of Fools: www.geocities.com/SoHo/Lofts/9367/
The Ooze: www.theooze.com
Beyond Magazine: www.beyondmag.com
Spirit Venture Ministries (Leonard Sweet): www.Leonardsweet.com
Phuture: www.phuture.org
21st Century Strategies Inc (Bill Easum): www.easum.com/
Third Way: www.thirdway.org.uk/
Zadok Perspectives: www.zadok.org.au

Postmodernism/Mission Principles

Young Leader Network: www.youngleader.org/postmodern.html

Anderson, W.T. *Reality Isn't What It Used To Be: Theatrical Politics, Ready-to-Wear Religion, Global Myths, Primitive Chic, and Other Wonders of the Postmodern World*, San Francisco: HarperCollins, 1990.
Bosch, D.J. *Transforming Mission: Paradigm Shifts in Theology of Mission*, Maryknoll: Orbis, 1991.
Connor, S. *Postmodernist Culture: An Introduction to Theories of the Contemporary*, Oxford: Blackwell, 1989.
Docker, J. *Postmodernism and Popular Culture: A Cultural History*, Cambridge: Cambridge University Press, 1994.
Featherstone, M. *Consumer Culture and Postmodernism*, London: Sage, 1991.

Grenz, Stanley. *A Primer on Postmodernism*, Grand Rapids, MI: Eerdmans, 1995.

Harvey, D. *The Condition of Postmodernity: An Enquiry into the Origins of Cultural Change*, Oxford: Blackwell, 1990.

Hilborn, David. *Picking Up the Pieces: Can Evangelicals Adapt to Contemporary Culture?* London: Hodder & Stoughton, 1997.

Lundin, R. *The Culture of Interpretation: Christian Faith and the Postmodern World*, Grand Rapids, MI: Eerdmans, 1993.

Middleton, J.R. and Walsh, BJ. *Truth Is Stranger Than It Used To Be: Biblical Faith in a Postmodern Age*, Downers Grove, IL: IVP, 1995.

Riddell, M. *Threshold of the Future: Reforming the Church in the Post-Christian West*, London: SPCK, 1998.

Walker, Andrew. *Telling the Story: Gospel, Mission and Culture*, London: SPCK, 1996.

The Bible in the Emerging Culture

Brueggemann, Walter. *Texts Under Negotiation: The Bible and Postmodern Imagination*, Minneapolis: Fortress, 1993.

Middleton, J.R. and Walsh, BJ. *Truth Is Stranger Than It Used To Be: Biblical Faith in a Postmodern Age*, Downers Grove, IL: IVP, 1995.

Riddell, Michael. *God's Home Page: A Journey Through the Bible for Postmodern Pilgrims*, London: Bible Reading Fellowship, 1998.

Strom, Mark. *Reframing Paul: Grace and Conversation - Then and Now*, IL: IVP, 2000.

Wink, Walter. *Transforming Bible Study*, Nashville: Abingdon Press, 1989.

Yancey, Philip. *The Jesus I Never Knew*, Grand Rapids, MI: Zondervan, 1995.

Labyrinths

Grace Cathedral (San Francisco): www.gracecathedral.org

Visions (York): www.abbess.demon.co.uk/visions/labyrinth.html

Artress, Lauren. *Walking a Sacred Path*, New York: Riverhead Books, 1995. (Available ex Grace Cathedral website above)

Prayers/Liturgy/Worship Resources

Writing Prayers: www.trinity-bris.ac.uk/altw_faq

Iona Community liturgy books: www.iona.org.uk.wgp/catalog.htm

Words From the Late Late Service: www.greenbelt.org.uk/altgrps/lls_word.htm

Anglican Prayerbook and Liturgy: www.ely.anglican.org/~sjk/liturgy/

Too Many Ands: Words for Worship from the Parallel Universe and Friends.
Email: info@cityside.org.nz
Duck, Ruth C. *Finding Words For Worship*, Louisville, Kentucky: Westminster
John Knox Press, 1995.

Music (Recorded)

Late Late Service: www.greenbelt.org.uk/altgrps/lls_music.html
Visions: www.abbess.demon.co.uk/visions
Suggested useable tracks: www.trinity-bris.ac.uk/altw_faq
New Zealand/Australian source for Late Late Service and other alt.worship
albums Email: info@cityside.org.nz
Turner, Steven. *Hungry for Heaven: Rock'n'Roll and the Search for
Redemption*, Downers Grove, IL: IVP, 2nd edn, rev., 1998.

Songs/Music

Iona/Wild Goose: www.iona.org.uk A large selection with a very wide range
of styles other than contemporary praise and worship. Excellent words,
often new lyrics to familiar tunes.

As One Voice songbooks and resources, published by Willow Connection,
Sydney. Fantastic stuff. Email: info@willowconnection.com.au
Order from: www.willowconnection.com.au

Video/Multimedia

Ginghamsburg Church. Website includes a large range of discussion groups,
practical tips and resources relating to the use of multimedia in worship:
www.ginghamsburg.org
Suggested use of and useable videos: www.trinity-bris.ac.uk/altw_faq
Wilson, Len. *The Wired Church*, Nashville: Abingdon Press, 1999.
Movies are reviewed from a Christian perspective at www.worshipworks.org
and the plots of thousands of movies can be found at us.imdb.com
One Small Barking Dog: producers of media resources:
www.osbd.org/index.html

Art/Images, Creativity and Imagination

Arts Centre Group: www2.greenbelt.org.uk/resource/acg.html
Brand, Hilary and Chaplin, Adrienne, *Art and Soul,* Cumbria (UK): Solway, 1999.

Contemplating Icons, St Pauls Multimedia Productions, 1989. UK: Middle
   Green, Slough SL3 6BS; USA: Heartbeat, PO Box 20, Donnellson, Iowa
   52625.   Fifty-minute video of Orthodox Icons with explanations.
Dillenberger, John. *A Theology of Artistic Sensibilities: The Visual Arts and
   the Church,* London: SCM, 1987.
De Oliveira, Nicholas et al. *Installation Art*, London: Thames & Hudson, 1996.
Fischer, Kathleen R. *The Inner Rainbow: The Imagination in Christian Life,*
   New Jersey: Paulist Press, 1983.

Worship and Mission in the Emerging Culture

Anderson, W. *Reality Isn't What It Used To Be: Theatrical Politics, Ready-to-
   Wear Religion, Global Myths, Primitive Chic, and Other Wonders of the
   Postmodern World*, San Francisco: Harper & Row, 1990.
Beaudoin, Tom.*Virtual Faith: The Irreverent Spiritual Quest of Generation X,*
   San Francisco: Jossey-Bass, 1998.
Bosch, David. *Transforming Mission: Paradigm Shifts in Theology of Mission,*
   Maryknoll, NY: Orbis, 1991.
Bosch, David. *Believing in the Future: Toward a Missiology of Western
   Culture*, Maryknoll, NY: Orbis, 1991.
Cray, Graham. *The Gospel and Tomorrow's Culture*, Warwick: CPAS, 1994.
Cray, Graham et al. *The Post-evangelical Debate,* London: SPCK, 1997.
Dawn, M. *Reaching Out Without Dumbing Down: A Theology of Worship for
   the Turn-of-the-Century Culture*, Grand Rapids, MI: Eerdmans, 1995.
Drane, John. *Faith in a Changing Culture: Creating Churches for the Next
   Century,* London: Marshall Pickering, 1997.
Drane, John. *Evangelism for a New Age: Creating Churches for the Next
   Century,* London: Marshall Pickering, 1994.
Fung, Raymond. *The Isaiah Vision,* Geneva: WCC, 1992.
Hilborn, David. *Picking Up the Pieces: Can Evangelicals Adapt to
   Contemporary Culture?,* London: Hodder & Stoughton, 1997.
Leech, Kenneth. *The Sky is Red: Discerning the Signs of the Times,* London:
   Darton, Longman & Todd, 1997.
Mead, Loren. *The Once and Future Church: Reinventing the Congregation for
   a New Mission Frontier,* New York: The Alban Institute, 1991.
Morganthaler, Sally. *Worship Evangelism,* Grand Rapids, MI: Zondervan, 1995.
Powell, Ruth and National Church Life Survey team. *Letter from Jen X,*
   Adelaide: Openbook, 2000.
Riddell, Michael. *Threshold of the Future: Reforming the Church in the Post-
   Christian West,* London: SPCK, 1998.

Roberts, Paul. *Alternative Worship in the Church of England*, Cambridge: Grove Books, 1999.

Sweet, Leonard. *SoulTsunami*, Grand Rapids, MI : Zondervan Publishing, 1999.

Sweet, Leonard. *AQUAChurch*, Colorado: Group Publishing, 1999.

Sine, Tom. *Mustard Seed vs McWorld: Reinventing Christian Life and Mission for a New Millennium*, Crowborough: Monarch Books, 1999.

Tomlinson, D. *The Post-Evangelical*, London: Triangle, 1995.

Ward, Peter. *Worship and Youth Culture*, London: Marshall Pickering, 1993.

Wuthnow, R. *Christianity in the 21st Century: Reflections on the Challenges Ahead*, Oxford: Oxford University Press, 1993.

What's Happening to the Church?

Kaldor, Peter. *National Church Life Survey: Shaping a Future: Characteristics of a Vital Congregation*, Adelaide: Openbook, 1997.

Kaldor, Peter and National Church Life Survey team: *Build my Church: Trends and Possibilities for Australian Churches*, Adelaide: Openbook, 1999.

Tomlinson, Dave. *The Post-Evangelical*, London: Triangle, 1995.

Cray, Graham et al. *The Post-evangelical Debate,* London: SPCK, 1997.

Space and Environments

Giles, Richard. *Re-pitching the Tent: Reordering the Church Building for Worship and Mission*, Norwich: Canterbury Press, 1999.

Spirituality and Faith Formation

Fowler, James. *Weaving the New Creation: Stages of Faith and the Public Church,* San Francisco: HarperCollins, 1991.

McLaren, Brian D. *Finding Faith: A Self-discovery Guide for Your Spiritual Quest,* Grand Rapids, MI: Zondervan, 1999.

Nouwen, Henri. *Life of the Beloved: Spiritual Living in a Secular World,* New York: Crossroad, 1993.

O'Donohue, John. *Anam Cara: Spiritual Wisdom from the Celtic World,* New York: Bantam Books, 1999.

Peck, M. Scott. *The Road Less Travelled: A New Psychology of Love, Traditional Values and Spiritual Growth,* London: Arrow Books, 1978.

Peterson, Eugene. *Subversive Spirituality,* Grand Rapids, MI: Eerdmans,, 1997.

Riddell, Mike. *Alt.Spirit@Metro.M3: Alternative Spirituality for the Third Millennium,* Oxford:Lion, 1997.

Riddell, Mike. *Godzone: A Guide to the Travels of the Soul,* Oxford: Lion, 1992.

Fiction

Costello, Tim. *Tips From a Travelling Soul Searcher*, Sydney: Allen and
   Unwin, 1999.
Coupland, D. *Generation X: Tales for an Accelerated Culture*, London:
   Abacus, 1991.
Coupland, D. *Life After God*, New York: Pocket books, Simon & Schuster, 1994.
Coupland, D. *Microserfs*, New York: Regan Books, HarperCollins, 1995.
Coupland, D. *Polaroids from the Dead*, New York: Regan Books,
   HarperCollins, 1996.
Coupland, D. *Girlfriend in a Coma*, London: Flamingo, 1998.
Gibson, W. *Neuromancer*, New York: Ace Books, 1984.
Gibson, W. *Count Zero*, New York: Arbor House, 1986.
Gibson, W. *Mona Lisa Overdrive*, New York: Bantam Books, 1988.

Gospel and Culture

Gilkey, L. *Society and the Sacred: Toward a Theology of Culture in Decline*,
   New York: Crossroad, 1981
Newbigin, L. *The Gospel in a Pluralist Society*, Grand Rapids, MI:
   Eerdmans, 1989.
Robinson, M. *The Faith of the Unbeliever: Building Innovative Relationships
   with The Unchurched*, Crowborough UK: Monarch, 1992.
Roxborough, A. *Reaching a New Generation: Strategies for Tomorrow's
   Church*, Downers Grove, IL: IVP, 1993.
Sine, T. *Wild Hope: Crises Facing the Human Community on the Threshold of
   the 21st Century*, Dallas: Word, 1991.
Wuthnow, R. *Christianity in the 21st Century: Reflections on the Challenges
   Ahead*, Oxford: Oxford University Press, 1993.

Courses

Spirituality and Creativity for Evangelism and Worship. Taught by John and
   Olive Drane at Fuller Seminary, Pasadena, California and in the UK.
New Ways of Worship and Mission in the Emerging Culture. Taught by Mike
   Riddell and Mark Pierson wherever it is requested.
   Email: info@cityside.org.nz

Various conferences on using multimedia in worship and related to doing
   church in the emerging culture are held in the USA. For example see
   www.ginghamsburg.org and www.Leonardsweet.com

LABYRINTHS – WALKING THE SACRED JOURNEY

Using the Labyrinth for Worship

BACKGROUND

A labyrinth is simply a path marked out on the ground that you walk around. In a Christian worship context a labyrinth is a path you walk as an aid to contemplation and reflection on God or on your relationship with God. Labyrinths are found in various religious traditions, not only Christian, and are pre-Christian in origin with the oldest surviving labyrinth being found in Sardinia and dating from 2500–2000 BCE.

A labyrinth is not a maze. It is unicursal, that is it has only one path, so you can't get lost. There are no choices to make about which path to take. No side roads or dead ends. No tricks. Just one path that leads you into the centre and back out again.

No one knows the origin of the labyrinth for sure. The oldest ones were small patterns carved on rocks, ceramics and clay tablets that were followed with a finger. The first walk-through construction was probably built in Egypt around 1800 BCE but it wasn't until 484 BCE that the term labyrinth first appeared, used by Herodotus.

They were, and are today, made of many materials – carved stone tracks, stones or shells to form the outline, mosaic tiles, mounds of grassed earth, plants or hedges, and most common today the very portable paint on canvas sheet.

Labyrinths were originally built to a formula using 'sacred geometry'. The same 'sacred geometry' of proportion, placement, position of stone, glass, wood and mortar, and system of angles, numbers and design, that were used to construct cathedrals and to place labyrinths within cathedrals. According to Lauren Artress[1] sacred geometry is a lost art today although it was once considered a divine art and master builders and masons were held in high esteem. Its purpose was to bring rest, comfort and harmony to the mind so that the mind could be open to other levels of awareness – to God.

DESIGNS

A variety of labyrinth designs exist. The two most useful are mentioned here: Chartres Labyrinth: This is the best-known and most popular labyrinth design. It also requires the largest area and is not easily reproducible or made to fit a given space. Drawing it requires some patience, skill and mathematical expertise.

You can purchase drawing kits and even completed labyrinths from 'The Labyrinth Project' at Grace Cathedral.[2] Many groups have made their own using a sketch as a guide.

Cretan Labyrinth: While not as interesting or as long, the advantages of this labyrinth are in its ease of construction and its ability to squeeze into small spaces. When using a labyrinth with a large group of people (say 20 or more) it can be helpful to have several smaller labyrinths to speed up the flow. I have drawn this shape with wool, flour, shells, rocks, sticky tape, as well as the usual paint on sheets. Creating it in advance is good, and making it together with the group who are going to walk it can also be great. It is a very versatile design and much more straightforward to draw than it first appears. Try it on a small piece of paper before you lay it out floor-sized! When setting it out note that the starting point is not the centre of the finished pattern, and in a tight space you should set the initial cross two-thirds to three-quarters of the way down the available space. The path width is set by where you place the second and third markers. This can be whatever distance suits you or your space. As little as 150mm (six inches) works fine if the group is small. It is helpful if you can create a 'bulge' in the centre space large enough for one or two people to sit or stand, or place a candle, a cross or other icon.

(See the 'Resources' section of the CD-ROM for diagrams.)

WALKING THE LABYRINTH

There are many ways to approach the labyrinth.

In the past people might walk it at some significant occasion such as the eve of their baptism, or in Holy Week as an aid to contemplative prayer and reflection. It can be seen as a centring exercise to help focus on God or as an allegory of your life – as you walk you sometimes find yourself close to God (the centre), only to then find yourself moving away from God (out on the edge). Likewise you will sometimes find yourself walking alongside someone, then meet them coming toward you, then see them again at some distance from you.

Another perspective would be to see the walking-in as walking toward God and walking-out as carrying Christ with you out into the world. You could build on that and use the walk-in to give an issue or concern over to God, the centre to reflect and receive, and the walk-out as the joining with God in working out the solution in the world.

You can use the journey to:
• Walk with God. Just relax, quieten your mind and listen to God as you walk.

- Repeat a phrase. For example the Jesus Prayer or a word or phrase of praise, request, repentance or something from the contemplative tradition.
- Request or question. You may take a question in with you, focusing on it or on talking to God about it as you walk. There is nothing magical about the labyrinth so your question should be outside the realm of yes and no answers.
- Pray.

The real beauty of the labyrinth is that it doesn't engage your rational mind. It connects with the more intuitive, symbolic, deeper mystery part of us and invites that side to respond. Which of course means that some people will not find the exercise of walking the labyrinth at all helpful. Remember that!

So the path winding around can become a mirror reflecting where we are in our lives and an allegory of where we are or would like to be with God. Note that because no one is imposing any particular content or outcome on the exercise of walking the labyrinth it is a safe place for people under stress or frightened or with a psychiatric illness.

The specific instructions for walking the labyrinth include …

1. Take off your shoes and step up to the labyrinth entrance. Pause and breathe deeply a few times. Centre yourself. Enter at the pace your body wants to go.
2. Stay on the path, i.e. the space between the lines. If you cross a line you change direction!
3. Look down, focus on the path. Move past people, overtake if you want to. Step aside to let another go past. Remember that those going out will meet those going in and vice versa.
4. Walk slowly. Place one foot in front of the other. Stepping in time to your breathing can be helpful.
5. When you reach the centre, stay there for a while. Notice the sensations in your body, your awareness … The centre is the place of resting with God.
6. Walk out when you are ready. The same pace and rules apply.

Talk to someone about your specific insights or experience if you need to.

A labyrinth is usually offered to people in the open-ended context of a two or three hour session where they can come and go as they wish to. It may begin with a brief introduction of the labyrinth but otherwise would allow people to participate in their own time and at their own pace. Don't overcrowd the labyrinth. Five to seven is probably enough in it at one time. You may want to walk through more than once.

FURTHER POSSIBILITIES

Music can (and probably should) be played in the background. We find that classical or chanting or ambient electronic type tracks work best. Something that doesn't have too much in the way of crescendos that disturb reflection, and isn't fast paced or too loud.[3] Long tapes can be achieved by copying tracks onto the soundtrack of a video tape. Live music is another possibility. Singing quietly together (unaccompanied) can be a wonderful experience.

The environment is very important and usually low light or candlelight works well. Icons or art works can be used as a focus for meditation and a candle or cross may also be placed in the centre of the labyrinth. I prefer an overall environment that is relatively uncluttered. The focus should be on reflection and meditation rather than on flashy images or lighting. One group set up various sensory experiences along the path of their labyrinth – a place to draw, somewhere to model clay, a tray of stones then of cotton wool to walk over. They also had a footwashing at the entrance. All with the objective of promoting some specific reflections on the journey theme. Incense, projected still images as a backdrop, even looped video images could all create a suitable overall environment.

Some discussion has occurred among us over whether or not we should make the communion elements available for people. Some think it is fitting to take bread and wine as a response, others see the solitary 'serve yourself' experience as the antithesis of the communal act of communion. I vacillate.

Consider forming a labyrinth in your home or outside in your garden, or in some public space like a park or car park. They don't have to be limited to church buildings.

FOOTNOTES

Chapter 2: What's Going On in the World?

1. Turning and turning in the widening gyre
   The falcon cannot hear the falconer;
   Things fall apart; the centre cannot hold;
   Mere anarchy is loosed upon the world...
   W.B. Yeats, 'The Second Coming' in R.J. Finneran (ed.), *The Poems of W.B. Yeats: A New Edition,* New York: Macmillan, 1924, p. 187.
2. 'In recent decades we have passed, like Alice slipping through the looking glass into a new world... It fills our daily lives with uncertainty and anxiety, renders us vulnerable to tyrants and cults, shakes religious faith, and divides societies into groups contending with one another in a strange and unfamiliar kind of ideological conflict: not merely conflict *between* beliefs, but conflict *about* belief itself.' Walter Truett Anderson, *Reality Isn't What It Used To Be: Theatrical Politics, Ready-to-Wear Religion, Global Myths, Primitive Chic, and Other Wonders of the Postmodern World,* San Francisco: Harper and Row, 1990, p. 3.
3. 'There are many people in the world who have been thus deeply dispossessed. You don't have to have left home to become a refugee.' Walter Truett Anderson, *Reality Isn't What It Used To Be: Theatrical Politics, Ready-to-Wear Religion, Global Myths, Primitive Chic, and Other Wonders of the Postmodern World,* San Francisco: Harper & Row, 1990, p. 27.
4. Indigenous people of Aotearoa/New Zealand.
5. 'This word has no meaning. Use it as often as possible.' Quoted in Mike Featherstone, *Consumer Culture and Postmodernism,* London: Sage, 1991, p. 1. Or again: 'Postmodernism is a contemporary movement. It is strong and fashionable. Over and above this, it is not altogether clear what the devil it is.' Ernst Gellner, *Postmodernism, Reason and Religion,* London: Routledge, 1992, p. 22.
6. Jacques Derrida, *Of Grammatology* (trans. G.C. Spivak), Baltimore: Johns Hopkins University Press, 1976; *Speech and Phenomena and Other Essays on Husserl's Theory of Signs* (trans. D.B. Allison), Evanston: Northwestern University Press, 1973; Jean François Lyotard, *The Postmodern Condition: A Report on Knowledge* (trans. G. Bennington and B. Massumi), Manchester: Manchester University Press, 1984; Jean Baudrillard, *The Mirror of Production* (trans. M. Poster), St Louis: Telos Press, 1975; *Simulations* (trans. P. Foss, P. Patton and P. Bleitchman), New York: Semiotext(e), 1983; Richard Rorty, *Philosophy and the Mirror of Nature,* Princeton: Princeton University Press, 1979; *Contingency, Irony, and Solidarity,* Cambridge: Cambridge University Press, 1989.
7. See, for example, Walter Truett Anderson, *Reality Isn't What It Used To Be:*

Theatrical Politics, Ready-to-Wear Religion, Global Myths, Primitive Chic, and Other Wonders of the Postmodern World, San Francisco: Harper & Row, 1990; Steven Connor, *Postmodernist Culture: An Introduction to Theories of the Contemporary,* Oxford: Blackwell, 1989; John Docker, *Postmodernism and Popular Culture: A Cultural History,* Cambridge: Cambridge University Press, 1994; Mike Featherstone, *Consumer Culture and Postmodernism,* London: Sage, 1991; David Harvey, *The Condition of Postmodernity: An Enquiry into the Origins of Cultural Change,* Oxford: Blackwell, 1990.

Chapter 4: New Approaches to Worship

1. 'The White Stone', Sacred Space Service by Dave Tomlinson and the Holy Joes crew at Greenbelt Festival, 1999.
2. alt.worship, alt.w, alternative worship, and new worship are all terms used interchangeably to describe the type of worship that is outside that usually experienced in mainstream churches. The kind of worship this Project is about. While none of the terms is perfect or liked universally, common usage means they have stuck.
3. Quoted in Martin Wroe (ed.), *God: What the Critics Say,* UK: Spire, 1992, p. 172.
4. Punter is a term commonly used in European and Australasian alternative worship circles to describe worshippers. It is a positive and widely inclusive description.
5. T. J. McNamara, Art Critic, *NZ Herald,* 27–28 February 1999, p.J9.
6. 'Rules of the Game', by Ralph Rugoff in *Friese* magazine, issue 44, 1999, pp. 46f.
7. Gene Edward Veith, *Guide to Contemporary Culture,* UK: Crossway Books, 1994, p. 93.
8. Brian Eno, 'Ambient Reflections', *Studio Sound* magazine (UK), October 1995.
9. Raymond Fung, *The Isaiah Vision,* Geneva: WCC, 1995, p. 13.
10. Sally Morgenthaler, *Worship Evangelism,* Michigan: Zondevan 1995, p. 30.
11. Gert Ruppell, *Ecumenical Letter on Evangelism 3,* Geneva: WCC, December 1995, p. 6.
12. Australia: Albatross Books, 1994, pp. 71f.
13. Quoted in *Third Way* magazine, April 1999, p. 5.
14. 'Culture Shock' seminar, Greenhouse, London, February 1993.
15. Simon Chaplin, Spine Community, Auckland, New Zealand.
16. Initially inspired by a conversation with Pete Ward.
17. Paradox Music, www.abbess.demon.co.uk/paradox/
18. See Chapter 6, 'Growing Edges', for '*The Story of Alt. Worship in Two Versions'*.
19. I'm indebted to John Hoyland for a posting on 5 June 1995 that first attempted to define these elements.

20. Interview by Sally Morgenthaler in *Worship Evangelism*, Michigan: Zondervan, 1995, p. 41.

21. *Words From the Late Late Service*, Glasgow: Late Late Service, 1993, p. 2.

22. Leonard Sweet, www.LeonardSweet.com ('Knowing the Times', June 1999). See 'Resources' for further materials.

23. Richard Giles, *Re-pitching the Tent: Reordering the Church Building for Worship and Mission*, Norwich: Canterbury Press, 1999, p. 57.

24. Doug Adams, *Involving the People in Dancing Worship: Historic and Contemporary Patterns*, Austin, Texas: The Sharing Company, 1975.

25. Thanks to Elaine Patterson, architect, Auckland, for initial ideas and stimulation to think about space and worship.

26. In the USA the films of some studios can be accessed through The Motion Picture Licencing Company.
Email: info@mplc.com

27. Richard Giles, *Re-pitching the Tent: Reordering the Church Building for Worship and Mission*, Norwich: Canterbury Press, 1999, p. 111.

28. www.epicentre.org.uk

29. The text of these readings is in the 'Resources' section: 'WORD, Liturgies'.

30. Mike Riddell, *Godzone: A Guide to the Travels of the Soul*, Oxford: Lion, 1992, pp. 90f.

31. Some of these are used on the CD-ROM.

32. Ruth C. Duck, *Finding Words For Worship*, Louisville, Kentucky: Westminster John Knox Press, 1995, p. 5.

33. Elizabeth O'Connor, *Eighth Day of Creation*, Waco, Texas: Word Books, 1971, p. 15.

34. Ruth C. Duck, *Finding Words For Worship*, Louisville, Kentucky: Westminster John Knox Press, 1995, p. 5.

Resources

1. Artress, Lauren. *Walking a Sacred Path*, New York: Riverhead Books, 1995. (Available ex Grace Cathedral website www.gracecathedral.org).

2. They also carry Artress's book and other labyrinth materials. www.gracecathedral.org

3. Late Late Service album 'Deep Peace', Grace album 'Eucharist', or any of the Visions albums can work well. See 'Music (Recorded)', and 'SOUND' in 'Resources' section of CD-ROM.

ABOUT THE CD

This CD works on Windows 95, 98, and NT 2000 (although we wrote it last century so it hasn't been tested for the new millennium), as well as with any PowerMac (including iMac). We recommend at least 32MB of RAM, speakers, and a video card that supports 800x600 resolution in 16-bit colour. In Windows, hide the task bar (it gets in the way).

The illuminated Prodigal Project should start automatically when you insert the CD. If it doesn't, use Find in the start menu, or Sherlock from the Apple menu, to locate the file called PRODIGAL. Double-click this file. If the video settings on your computer are inadequate, or if QuickTime has not been installed on your system, The Prodigal Project will warn you, and give you some help. Apart from QuickTime, nothing new will be installed on your computer's hard drive. The Prodigal Project program runs entirely from the CD.

The text of the book is reproduced on the CD, which also has more to offer: more stories in 'Hopeful Rumours', and more poems and liturgies in 'Resources'.

To exit the Project, locate and click the button at bottom right of the screen. This will take you to the Credits screen, from which you'll have to click the exit button again. To quit immediately, press ESC (escape) at any time.

The Prodigal Project has an 'automatic mode', in which The Project flips randomly through screens and animations.Press 'Shift A' at any time to activate (and deactivate) this mode.

As an alternative to the mouse, use the cursor keys on the right-hand side of the keyboard. Up and down arrows scroll text. 'PageUp' and 'PageDown' jumps to the top and bottom of text; and right and left arrows move forward and back through the chapter.

Explore. Click on everything. Look and listen.
There are hidden corners.

Don't forget the automatic mode for the
window display in your bookshop!

Can't work out how to use the CD? Email andrew at: lorien@zeta.org.au
Browse through our updates and other info at www.prodigal-project.com